THE OFFICIAL
BLUE JAYS
ALBUM

The Official Blue Jays Album

A Dozen Years of Baseball Memories

Ken Fidlin & Fred Thornhill

A Lorraine Greey Book

Seal Books

The Author

Ken Fidlin writes a daily baseball column for *The Toronto Sun*. He has covered the Blue Jays for the *Sun* since 1983.

The Photographer

Fred Thornhill is a staff photographer with *The Toronto Sun*. He has photographed the Blue Jays for both the *Sun* and the Toronto Blue Jays Public Relations Department.

A Lorraine Greey Book

Canadian Cataloguing in Publication Data

Fidlin, Ken
The official Blue Jays album

ISBN 0-7704-2316-7

1. Toronto Blue Jays (Baseball team) – History.
I. Thornhill, Fred. II. Title.

GV875.T6F52 1989 796.357'64'09713541
C89-093137-2

Published by
Seal Books
McClelland-Bantam Inc.
105 Bond Street
Toronto, Ontario
M5B 1Y3 Canada

Produced for Seal Books by
Lorraine Greey Publications Limited
56 The Esplanade, Suite 303
Toronto, Ontario
M5E 1A7 Canada

Designed by Don Fernley and Emma Hesse

Printed in Canada

Acknowledgements

We would like to thank Randy Echlin for permitting us to pick and choose from his treasure trove of Blue Jays memorabilia for the material shown in the cover photograph. Thanks also to Patrick Grier for his many hours of research.

K.F. & F.T.

Photo Credits

Stan Behal/Canada Wide — 92, 116 (bottom)
Norm Betts/Canada Wide — 8, 11, 18, 21 (top)
Canada Wide — 10, 29, 30, 32, 34, 38 (top), 53, 60, 83
Mike Cassese/Canada Wide — 127
Barry Gray/Canada Wide — 41, 52
Gary Hershorn — 44 (left), 87
Julien LeBourdais — 16, 19, 20, 21 (bottom)
Bill Majesky/Canada Wide — 93 (bottom)
Mike Peake/Canada Wide — 6-7
Fred Thornhill — 1, 5, 47, 62, 106 (top), 111, 114, 118, 128
Fred Thornhill/Blue Jays — 2, 39, 42, 50, 68, 69, 73, 76, 98, 102, 103, 104, 106 (bottom), 108, 112, 120, 124
Fred Thornhill/Canada Wide — 55, 58, 61, 66, 74, 78, 80, 82, 84, 88, 91, 93, 94, 96, 100, 116 (top), 125
Toronto Blue Jays — 14, 22, 26, 31, 44 (right), 46, 54
Hugh Wesley/Canada Wide — 38 (bottom), 57, 64

Cover photography by Clive Webster/Format

Page 2: *Although Dave Stieb has always been one of the more controversial Jays, there's no questioning his success. He's won more games than any other Toronto pitcher.*

Page 5: *B.J. Birdie has been leading the cheers at Exhibition Stadium since 1977.*

Pages 6-7: *Doyle Alexander rode above a sea of teammates and fans after defeating the New York Yankees 5-1 on October 5, 1985, and winning Toronto's first American League East division championship.*

CONTENTS

INTRODUCTION 9

1977 – OPENING DAY 17

1978 – THE TERRIBLE TWOS 27

1979 – GROWING PAINS 35

1980 – A NEW ERA 43

1981 – LOSERS, ALL 51

1982 – A NEW ATTITUDE 59

1983 – GREAT EXPECTATIONS 67

1984 – THE TIGERS ROAR 77

1985 – THAT CHAMPIONSHIP SEASON 85

1986 – HEADING FOR A FALL 99

1987 – BEST OF TIMES, WORST OF TIMES 109

1988 – A SUMMER OF DISCONTENT 121

BLUE JAY

Best Built
North American Cars
1985
EAST DIVISION
CHAMPIONS
4:29
Coke

INTRODUCTION

In the summer of 1985 a schoolteacher named Bob Wood set out from Seattle on a two-month odyssey that took him to every one of baseball's twenty-six parks. The result of his trip was a book, *Dodger Dogs to Fenway Franks*, in which he described the nuances of each stadium. In the end, he rated the parks based on a variety of criteria: seating, atmosphere, food, facilities, layout and so on.

It will come as a shock to no one in Toronto that Exhibition Stadium ranked twenty-sixth out of twenty-six. For years Torontonians had known theirs was the worst baseball stadium in the major leagues, and now those suspicions had been verified by an independent inquiry.

In the summer of 1989 the Blue Jays leave this squalor and move into the twenty-first century. The SkyDome, their new home, is everything Exhibition Stadium was not. The new place simply oozes comfort and convenience, glitter and pizzazz, sunshine with a roof over your head. It may well become the benchmark by which future stadiums are judged.

But homely old Exhibition Stadium has what the SkyDome can never possess: priceless memories of the birth, nurturing and blossoming of major-league baseball in Toronto. It is the place where, in a freak spring blizzard, the Blue Jays took their first stumbling steps down the road to respectability, and it is the place where champagne flowed like water in October, 1985. In the mind's eye, it is the place of Doug Ault just as it is the place of Fred McGriff.

Shortly after he was hired on June 18, 1976, executive vice-president Peter Bavasi proudly showed off the team's assets: two paper clips.

The fact is that thirteen years after their birth the Blue Jays are as inextricably woven into the fabric of life in Toronto as the Tigers are in Detroit or the Red Sox are in Boston. It did not take a hallowed old shrine like Tiger Stadium or Fenway Park to accomplish that, either.

Way back when, Exhibition Stadium was simply a place to play, a carrot to draw major-league baseball to Metro Toronto. It served its purpose well. By the

end of the 1988 season 22,465,106 fans had paid their way in to watch Blue Jays baseball over the course of twelve seasons.

Rookie manager Roy Hartsfield surveys his team's renovated ball park in the fall of 1976.

♦ FIRST THINGS FIRST

"Son, I'll tell you how it works. First you've got to build us a stadium, then baseball will decide whether or not you get a team." That was the voice of Baseball Commissioner Bowie Kuhn, over a drink in a Florida hotel lounge, imparting the facts of life to a North York alderman in 1972. The alderman was Paul Godfrey, and he was determined that sooner, rather than later, baseball would come to Toronto.

For several years Godfrey had been enthralled with the notion of a big-league baseball team in Toronto. In North York he had been involved in a group that tried to get financing for a domed stadium, and he often travelled at his own expense to places that he knew baseball executives were gathering in hopes his presence would lead to a franchise for Metro.

By 1973 Godfrey was in a position of power and authority as Chairman of Metropolitan Toronto. On the day of the Grey Cup game that year, while Godfrey and Ontario Premier William Davis stood shuffling their feet at midfield, waiting for Governor General Roland Michener to arrive for the ceremonial kickoff, Godfrey sprang his plan on the premier. "I think we should build a baseball stadium right here," said Godfrey, describing a new set of angled stands to the south that would accommodate both baseball and football.

The seeds were planted. It wasn't long before Godfrey had a commitment from the municipal government for half the money. With some reluctance the province eventually came up with the rest of the complicated financial package.

The Blue Jays brain trust checks some last-minute details before the expansion draft on November 5, 1976. From left: Bobby Prentice, Elliott Wahle, Bob Miller, Pat Gillick, Roy Hartsfield, Bobby Mattick and Al LaMacchia.

The existing south stands were torn down and replaced by a continuous set of stands that wrapped around home plate at the southwest corner of the field and down the third-base line, creating 33,000 baseball seats with perhaps 20,000 more in the north grandstand. It was a $17.8-million gamble.

In retrospect, it was a bargain. The stadium expansion price tag has been repaid many times over. "The mandate," says architect Bill Sanford, who redesigned the stadium, "was to make it last for approximately ten years for $15 million, and no one has ever done that unless you go way back to the early days of stadiums. I think the taxpayers have had a really fair shake."

♦ PRIMING THE PUMP

But in those days, with no firm baseball prospects lined up, there were plenty of sceptics. With construction under way, the campaign to attract either an existing team or a new franchise to Toronto began to heat up.

Near the end of 1974 Labatt Breweries of Canada Ltd. entered the fray. "We wanted to move our brewery onto centre stage in Toronto," said then-president Don McDougall, the driving force in the movement. "A baseball team was the best promotional vehicle available." McDougall, a native of Prince Edward Island, was a former teacher and air force officer, the son of a Canadian National Railway station-agent. At thirty-five he was the youngest president in Labatt's history. "I'd never even seen a major-league baseball game," he said. "This was business. Purely business."

By now, no baseball meeting could be held without someone — Godfrey or McDougall or lawyer Herb Solway, or sometimes all three — on hand to sell Toronto. Finally, late in 1975, someone was prepared to listen.

Horace Stoneham, the owner of the San Francisco Giants, was in deep financial misery, reportedly $2 million in debt. About this time financier Howard Webster and the Canadian Imperial Bank of Commerce joined the Labatt group to create a bidder with tremendous financial wallop. Labatt Breweries and Webster, who counted among his assets *The Globe and Mail*, were in for forty-five percent each. The bank had a ten-percent share.

Early in 1976 a deal was struck. The Labatt group would pay $8 million for the Giants and another $5.5 million to cover the remaining nineteen years on the lease at Candlestick Park. The sale was announced at a news conference in Toronto, and hats emblazoned with the new Toronto Giants logo were distributed.

But the deal fell through. San Francisco Mayor George Moscone and National League President Chub Feeney, a San Francisco resident, joined forces to block the sale. A California judge issued a temporary restraining order, blocking the move and buying time to find a backer who would keep the team in San Francisco.

Two hours before the deadline, with the Giants apparently headed for Toronto, a partnership between West Coast entrepreneur Bob Lurie and a Phoenix meat packer named Bud Herseth came up with the $8 million. The Giants would stay in San Francisco.

♦ BASEBALL'S BACK IN TOWN

Things moved quickly after that, despite the setback. The San Francisco disappointment was still fresh when the American League decided to expand. Seattle would get one franchise because the league feared losing a lawsuit brought by the city when the Pilots deserted them for Milwaukee in 1970. Toronto was prime territory for the other one.

Suddenly the National League was interested, as well, and Toronto, rather than chasing baseballs, was now at bat. On March 20, 1976, by a vote of eleven to one, the American League awarded Toronto the second franchise. The National League countered by suggesting that Toronto and Washington be awarded National League franchises and that the American League could find another city to go along with Seattle.

But when no financial backer could be found for Washington, and when the National League, which needed a unanimous consent, could not decide, Kuhn finally dismissed the National League's objections. Toronto and Seattle were in the American League and would begin play in April, 1977.

So much to do and so little time. In May a chartered accountant, the friend of a friend of McDougall's named Paul Beeston, was hired to handle the purse strings. A boisterous, cigar-chomping native of Welland, Ontario, Beeston defied all the accountant stereotypes.

The next step was to find a general manager, a special job requiring special skills. The successful candidate obviously had to have a thorough knowledge of baseball. But he also had to have a dynamic personality and be a consummate salesman. The man McDougall settled upon to oversee the big picture was Peter Bavasi.

♦ EIGHT-YEAR TIMETABLE

Peter Bavasi's childhood was every little boy's dream. The Brooklyn Dodgers' dugout was his playpen. People like Jackie Robinson, PeeWee Reese, Preacher Roe, Roy Campanella, Gil Hodges and Johnny Podres, heroic figures to Bavasi's generation, were simply "the guys."

Peter was born on Halloween in 1942, the son of E.J. "Buzzie" Bavasi, the general manager of the legendary Bums of Flatbush, and his earliest baseball recollections are not of wins and losses, homers and strikeouts, but of dollars and cents. "In our house there was the ever-prevailing sense of the business of baseball," he said in a 1976 interview. "I was always more concerned with how a baseball team was put on the field, what was happening behind the scenes, rather than who was on first or what somebody's batting average was."

By his own description "a mediocre player," Bavasi graduated from St. Mary's College in Moraga, California, in 1964 and signed on as the business manager of the Dodgers' AAA farm club in Albuquerque. After several years at various minor-league posts he joined his father in San Diego with the expansion Padres. Four years later he became the Padres' vice-president and general manager.

Bavasi was hired at a salary of $65,000 annually on a five-year contract and immediately set up shop in room 429 of the Lord Simcoe Hotel, since demolished. He pushed hard those early years, and in pushing hard he inevitably rubbed some people the wrong way. Under his stewardship the team broke all existing expansion attendance records while playing in a less-than-perfect stadium. In addition, his marketing schemes netted huge financial gains as he flogged the Blue Jays' logo all over Canada, on shirts, mugs, caps, lunch pails and pennants.

He generated plenty of press, both good and bad. It seemed he was one of those people who was either loved or hated. And he could be feisty.

Bavasi was awakened from sleep past midnight one night in 1979 by a call from a reporter from *The Toronto Star*.

"What are you doing?" asked the reporter.

"I was sleeping," Bavasi shrieked. "What kind of stupid question is that?"

The reporter wanted to know about a rumor that manager Roy Hartsfield had been fired. No, he had not.

Bavasi could not get back to sleep. Finally he telephoned *The Star* newsroom and asked politely for the phone number of Martin Goodman, the president of *The Star*.

A few moments later Goodman's phone rang, pulling him out of a deep sleep.

"Hi, it's Pete Bavasi. What are you doing, Marty?"

"Sleeping," cried Goodman.

Roy Hartsfield had some trying times during his three-year tenure as the Blue Jays' manager.

"That's what I was doing until one of your reporters woke me up at one o'clock. And you know what? Now that I have your home phone number, I am going to call you every middle of the night that *The Star* calls me."

When he had finally worn out his welcome, Bavasi needed little nudging to move on. That came at the end of his fifth year, in the fall of 1981. "Pro sport is like a train where, sooner or later, the conductor comes down the aisle to punch your ticket," he said. "If you really plan it well, you can leap off that train a moment before he gets to you. Sooner or later he does, and it's better to go gracefully and quickly before he gets to you."

But in that summer of 1976 the conductor hadn't even reported for work. In fact, Bavasi's ball team didn't even know what to call itself.

♦ THE DINGBATS?

The new team needed a name, and it went to the people to get one. A name-the-team contest produced 30,000 responses from which a "short list" of 4,000 names was selected. Among the losers: Les Battes Bleus, Foresters, Orbits, Mounties, 77s, Lumberjacks, Blue Sox, Blue Shoes, Blue Birds, Blazing Bats, Towers, Trilliums, Toronto Island Ferries, Shamrocks, Beavers, Preachers, Pastors and Rabbis — even Dingbats. There were seventy-three different varieties of animals and forty-six different types of birds among the entries.

On 154 ballots, though, appeared the name "Blue Jays," and it was one of ten that were sent to the team's board of directors for a final decision.

"The Blue Jay is a North American bird indigenous to the Ontario region," said Bavasi when the choice was announced. "It's feisty and aggressive, the kind of ball club we hope to field for the fans in Toronto. The colors also match those of the other Toronto teams."

Pat Gillick, vice-president of player personnel, was on staff by mid-August, lured away from the Yankees by the challenge of building a big-league baseball program from scratch. While Bavasi retained the title of general manager, it was clear that the baseball operation was Gillick's baby.

Next on the list of priorities was a manager. Bavasi opted for a man he knew and respected. When Bavasi had taken that first job out of college in 1964, Roy Hartsfield had been the Albuquerque manager. Hartsfield had so impressed Bavasi that he told him if the opportunity ever presented itself he would hire Hartsfield to manage in the big leagues.

♦ "I KNOW I CAN DO IT."

Almost thirteen years later, Bavasi made good on his promise. On September 22, 1976, Roy Hartsfield was appointed the first manager of the Toronto Blue Jays. Over the next three years the fifty-year-old Georgia native would suffer every frustration imaginable to a baseball manager, but with fifteen years' minor-league experience already under his belt, there wasn't that much left to shock or dismay Hartsfield. All but three of his eighteen years as a player had been spent in the minor leagues. He had managed to hang on for three seasons (1950-52) with the Boston Braves, but he didn't retire officially until 1961. At that time he'd already been a player-manager for three years. His managerial career took him to eight cities in sixteen years, the last four with the Hawaii Islanders.

"I know I can do it," said Hartsfield that day. "The game itself is the same whether it's Triple-A ball or the major leagues. There's still ninety feet between the bases."

A month later, on October 21 — two weeks before the expansion draft — the Jays purchased their first player. He was a catcher named Phil Roof, thirty-five years old and a veteran of twelve years with seven major-league teams. He was purchased from the Chicago White Sox. "We intend to draft young players, especially pitchers. Therefore, we figure a veteran catcher will be a helpful instructor for a young staff and be able to provide game leadership," explained Bavasi.

On draft day, November 5, 1976, after Seattle had selected outfielder Ruppert Jones from Kansas City, Bob Bailor was the first of thirty selections by the Jays from players made available by the rest of the American League. Bailor, an infielder left unprotected by the Baltimore Orioles, was followed, in order, by pitcher Jerry Garvin, pitcher Jim Clancy, outfielder Gary Woods, first baseman Rico Carty and pitcher Butch Edge.

At the end of the day the Jays announced their first trade, dealing away pitcher Al Fitzmorris to the Cleveland Indians for catcher Alan Ashby and first baseman Doug Howard.

Of the sixty players obtained that day, just three — Ernie Whitt, Jim Clancy and Dave Collins — were still active at the end of the 1988 season.

1977

OPENING DAY

Let's face it. The SkyDome is to Exhibition Stadium what the space shuttle is to the biplane: linked by the bonds of evolution but still worlds apart. Yet no matter how richly appointed the new Blue Jays' nest, no matter how anxious we are to show it off to the world and no matter how extravagant the housewarming party, it will never compare with that wacky April afternoon in 1977 spent on frozen metal benches.

Opening day. From San Diego to Chicoutimi, Key West to Kelowna, those two words have a singularly romantic ring tinged with special private memories. There is no symbol of annual renewal more poignant to a baseball fan than the rebirth that comes with opening day.

♦ BEGINNINGS

Between them, Pat Gillick and his assistant, Elliott Wahle, had left few avenues unexplored in their search for players who might be able to help as that first spring training approached.

Born in the Bronx, Wahle worked in the front office for the Yankees in the early seventies and was a close friend of Gillick's. When the Jays offered Gillick a job, he convinced Wahle to come with him.

Most of the players had been recruited through the expansion draft. Others, like infielder Pedro Garcia, had been signed as free agents, and some, like veteran catcher Phil Roof, had been purchased from other organizations.

It was snowy and cold on opening day, 1977, but Toronto's baseball fans were all smiles.

As can be expected in a fledgling enterprise of such high profile, Wahle received many impassioned letters from men pleading for an opportunity to get in on the ground floor. He kept a file of them. "An ardent baseball fan from childhood," wrote one man, "I have, like many others, dreamt of playing major-league baseball. I have kept myself in superb physical condition. I have never smoked, I abstain from drinking hard liquor and, being the captain of a

steamship vessel, my wife and two children are used to my being away from home." Admirable qualities, Wahle conceded, but not necessarily those required of a major-league baseball player.

"I swear to God," wrote another, "that I can play ball with anyone, and that's what I want to do. I've never begged for anything in my entire life, but I'm begging you now to give me an opportunity to play pro ball. Please help me!"

When they had separated, as best they knew how, the prospects from the impostors, Gillick and Wahle were left with a roster of seventeen pitchers, four catchers, ten infielders and seven outfielders. Thirty-eight players in all would report to spring training in Dunedin, Florida.

It was a beginning.

Throughout the spring, as anticipation built in Toronto, the Canadian public devoured every bit of information about this collection of strangers about to drop into their midst. The team played twenty-four games in Florida, winning only eight. By the end of March, Harrah's in Reno posted somewhat conservative 500-to-1 odds against Toronto's winning the American League pennant. But the team's immediate potential didn't matter. All that mattered was that baseball was coming to town.

♦ A BLIZZARD OF EMOTIONS

Thursday, April 7, 1977. An afternoon cold enough to freeze dozens of images for all time. Not just opening day. The first opening day.

In reality, the ugly football-cum-baseball stadium on the shore of icy Lake Ontario had all the atmosphere of a parking garage. But on that day it was our own Fenway Park. Our own Wrigley Field.

And the memories return in a flood. . . .

Left: *At the opening of the team's first training camp, Roy Hartsfield laid down the law: no beards, no mustaches, no jeans.*

Right: *Al Woods strapped on the boards before the first game.*

The forecast was for snow and freezing temperatures, and for once the weather predictors had got it right.

"It's J-Day — And Snow," barked the headline in a morning paper. Indeed, as game time approached and the stands began to fill with fans in parkas and snowmobile suits, the skies were forbidding and the temperature sat precisely at the freezing point.

"We want beer!" chanted the fans, underscoring that Exhibition Stadium was the one baseball park out of twenty-six in the majors that did not allow the sale of beer. It would take four years for the fans' persistence to be rewarded.

When umpire Nestor Chylak noted that Chicago lead-off man Ralph Garr was ready, he stepped in behind catcher Rick Cerone. Chylak signalled to pitcher Bill Singer and crisply instructed the Blue Jays and Chicago White Sox to "Play ball!" A moment later, as snowflakes settled to earth all around him, Singer painted the corner of the plate with a fastball strike, and as the crowd roared in the beginning of a new era on the Toronto sporting scene, the dream became reality. The ball was removed from the game, and is now on display at the Baseball Hall of Fame in Cooperstown, New York.

Garr walked. Two outs later — one of them a run-scoring sacrifice fly by Jorge Orta — Chicago's Richie Zisk felt that unmistakably satisfying jolt as bat squarely met ball. Blue Jays fans had just seen their first home run and known their first heartache as Chicago took a 2-0 lead.

Snow fell and stayed, creating a bizarre Christmassy scene sure to be a hit on the evening news in Miami, Dallas and Los Angeles. The afternoon became a cross between the traditional American summer game and the traditional Canadian winter carnival.

A twenty-seven-year-old Texan named Doug Ault, a player of modest talent

Otto Velez out-muscled Mike Willis (left) and Pedro Garcia for a prime seat in front of the heater on opening day.

but possessing a flare for the dramatic, became an immediate folk hero when he answered Zisk's homer with two of his own. One came in the bottom of the first inning, the other came in the bottom of the third to tie it. "I hope nobody pinches me and wakes me up," said Ault after the game. "After I hit those two out, I couldn't believe it was that easy."

By the game's end, 202 minutes after Singer's historic first pitch, seven pitchers had surrendered thirty-one hits and the Jays had a 9-5 win. Euphoric fans chanting "We're number one!" signalled the immediate emotional bond that had developed between themselves and this band of castoffs.

Ault had already found his way into their hearts, and others would follow.

On a mantle of white, the Blue Jays and White Sox brought baseball to Toronto on April 7, 1977.

Pitcher Bill Singer delivered the first pitch — a strike.

BLUE JAY

Otto Velez — "Otto the Swatto" as the ex-Yankee became known — was wielding a hot bat in those early days, hammering five homers and driving in eighteen runs in April. His .442 batting average earned him player-of-the-month honors in the American League. More than that, he lent an air of legitimacy to a franchise still looking for self-confidence. On his first return visit to Yankee Stadium that month, Velez left his former teammates a memorable calling card with nine hits — including two homers — in fifteen at-bats over four games.

Likewise, left-handed pitcher Jerry Garvin emerged quickly as a fan favorite, rolling up a perfect 4-0 April record as the Jays finished the month at 10-11, just one game under .500.

But a baseball season is a marathon, not a sprint. Their early success was soon spent, and by May 25 the team had finally found its level. On that day they lost a heartbreaker, 6-5 in ten innings against the Oakland Athletics, to fall into seventh and last place for the very first time.

Over the course of the next six years of wandering in baseball's wilderness, seventh place became one of the few things the team could count on.

♦ "YOU BIN DRAFTED!"

One of the players who gave fans hope for the future was Bob Bailor. In many respects "Buzz" represented the master plan that Gillick felt would eventually get the team to the top.

Bailor was a young, aggressive player with a burning desire to win. He had speed and solid defensive skills, but it was his determination that had kept his dream alive year after year in the Baltimore Orioles' chain. "I spent seven years in the minor leagues, and every year Baltimore kept protecting me," said Bailor. "They kept telling me I was doing well and then leaving me down there. I figured the only reason I stayed around that long was because I tried harder than anybody else."

Robert Michael Bailor was born June 10, 1951, in the town of Connellsville, Pennsylvania, once a bustling railroad and mining centre located in the foothills of the Appalachian Mountains about fifty miles southeast of Pittsburgh.

His father, Bob Sr., now retired, worked for the railroad as did his father and his father's father before that. "My grandfather came out from Poland," the elder Bob said in a 1977 interview, "and the only work goin' was on the railroad. But his name was Balgosky, and he found out fast that the big shots runnin' the railroad would hardly let you in the front door if you were a foreigner. So my grandfather learned English the best he could and gave himself the name Bailor because someone down the street had it and he liked its sound. He got the job, and we been a railroadin' family ever since."

Versatile Bob Bailor personified the type of team Pat Gillick wanted to build: young, fast and aggressive.

Bob was the oldest of four children, and when he was born in 1951, Bob Sr. immediately went out and bought a bat, glove and a ball. "Once introduced to sports, I never had to push him," said his dad. "When Bob was hardly able to walk, he wanted me to go out in the snow and play catch with him."

Still, young Bob was not so outstanding that the major-league scouts were breaking down his door after high school. Finally, when he'd all but given up on the idea of a career in baseball, the Baltimore Orioles signed him.

He rose steadily through the Baltimore chain until he arrived at Rochester, the Orioles' top farm team in the International League. At the end of the 1975 season the Orioles called him up for five games, and Bailor began to think his big-league dream was close at hand.

That winter, however, while playing winter ball in Venezuela, Bailor's throwing arm started to betray him. "I hadn't thrown a ball for three months, and they put me at second base, a position I wasn't used to. Suddenly my shoulder was sore."

Through the tail end of the 1976 season the Blue Jays were frantically scouting players for the upcoming expansion draft. Bailor, because of his bad shoulder, was a prime candidate to go unprotected by the Orioles, and the Jay brass knew it. Gillick and scout Al LaMacchia took a long, hard look at Bailor during Instructional League workouts following the '76 season.

"I watched his eyes," LaMacchia told columnist Trent Frayne. "That's how you know if someone's hurting — the eyes. If a ball player has to make a tough throw, he'll wince if it hurts."

Bailor didn't wince and thus became Toronto's number-one pick in the expansion draft. Not once has the team regretted it.

"Me, my best buddy, Mike, and my brother 'Woo' were just comin' home with some wild turkeys we shot for Thanksgiving, and we saw Dad standing on the porch a-hollerin' and a-yellin' and jumpin' up and down. 'Hurry up,' he's shoutin'. 'We just got the news. You bin drafted number one by them Toronto Blue Jays.' Dad, he was so damn happy. It was the best Thanksgiving we ever had," Bailor told *Canadian* magazine.

By the end of that first season in Toronto he had established himself not only as the team's most valuable player, but also as the most versatile, able to play both the outfield and infield. His .310 batting average is the best ever by a player on an expansion team. While Baltimore's Eddie Murray was named rookie of the year in the American League, Bailor, Ault and Garvin were all included on the annual all-rookie all-star team.

That first season Bob Bailor embodied everything the fans loved about the Blue Jays. "I had to work to be average," says Bailor. That may be true but those fledgling Jays had to work hard even to be below average.

♦ THE SEEDS ARE SOWN

Still, there were some memorable days that first year. On September 10, just three days after being chewed out publicly by Bavasi for playing "dead-ass baseball," the team responded with a stunning 19-3 defeat of the Yankees, New York's worst defeat in fifty-two years at Yankee Stadium. Roy Howell knocked in nine runs that day, a team record that still stands.

"I was thinking," said manager Hartsfield after the game, "that maybe the league should allow expansion teams one concession — when we win like this, we should be allowed to put our excess runs into a reservoir and use them at a later date."

Pete Vuckovich, who went on to become a Cy Young award winner as a starting pitcher in Milwaukee in 1982, was a pleasant surprise for the Jays in '77. He both started and relieved successfully. He pitched the team's first shutout (2-0 over Baltimore on June 26) and in the process he struck out a record-breaking twelve men.

Bill Singer, the pitcher who threw the first pitch in the opening day game, proved as disappointing as the season for the Blue Jays. Once a twenty-game winner with the Dodgers and Angels, Singer developed back problems with the Jays and never really helped them that much, appearing in just thirteen games, winning two of them. By the end of the year, he retired.

His name still comes up often in conversation, though, when people are talking about Blue Jays' trades. It turns out that Gillick had worked out a deal with the Yankees: Bill Singer for a young, unknown left-hander named Ron Guidry. Bavasi quashed the deal, feeling that Singer was one of the few recognizable players on the team. Guidry, of course, went on to become one of the premier pitchers in the game.

Through all the pain and frustration of building a team from nothing, the Jays remained a huge success at the box office. Bavasi's brilliant marketing technique — "selling the sizzle without the steak" — worked magnificently. They finished that first season with the absolute worst record in baseball, 54 wins and 107 losses, yet they smashed all existing attendance records for an expansion team.

♦ NO DOUBTS REMAIN

For all its warts, Exhibition Stadium hosted 1,701,052 baseball fans, about a half-million more than went to see the Expos in their first season of operation. Any lingering doubts about Toronto's ability to support major-league baseball had been erased.

More important, the seeds that would eventually make the team a contender had been sown. By the end of 1977 names like Jim Clancy, Ernie Whitt and Garth Iorg were already well known within the organization. Seventy-seven of Toronto's 107 losses had been by one- or two-run deficits, an encouraging sign. "If those seventy-seven games had been decided by ten or twelve runs, I'd feel a helluva lot worse than I do now," said Hartsfield when assessing the season. And down below, the farm system was about to start percolating.

One date in particular stands out as a link between the Jays of then and the Jays of now. On June 8, in the middle of their expansion blues, the Jays were being rudely treated by California Angels star Nolan Ryan. He struck out nineteen Jays that night en route to a 2-1 victory. Thousands of miles away, unnoticed and just a little fearful of what the future held, Jesse Barfield was preparing to leave home for the uncertainty of a life in baseball. Still just seventeen, Barfield had signed with the Blue Jays.

JAYS

1978

THE TERRIBLE TWOS

As an expansion team built from the culls of the established clubs, the Blue Jays knew from the beginning the road to respectability would be long and occasionally discouraging. While other teams were replenishing themselves from farm systems established decades before, the Toronto club had nowhere to turn. They bit the bullet and again lost more than a hundred games, a milestone in futility.

Still, Toronto fans found plenty to cheer about among their lovable losers. They had Rico Carty, "The Beeg Mon," and Bob Bailor, "The Leetle Mon." One day while Bailor was being interviewed on television, Carty walked up behind him and rested his chin on Bailor's head. "This is The Beeg Mon speaking to you live from behind The Leetle Mon," he said, cracking up the TV crew.

There were some bright spots to be sure. Bailor continued to shine, hitting .264 and driving in fifty-two runs while scoring seventy-four times to earn his second straight player-of-the-year award. Third baseman Roy Howell hit .270 with sixty-one RBIs. John Mayberry hit twenty-two homers, and Rico Carty stroked twenty more. Jim Clancy emerged as the ace of the pitching staff, and reliever Victor Cruz had a sensational year, winning seven games and saving nine in a season that produced very few save opportunities.

Rico Carty, "The Beeg Mon," hit twenty homers for Toronto in 1978, then stroked eleven more for Oakland after a mid-August trade.

But the team still lost 102 games and finished 40 games distant from the division champion Yankees. While that can hardly be viewed as a positive achievement, the Blue Jays were indeed growing by leaps and bounds in a variety of unseen ways.

From the very beginning upper management knew that patience would be necessary. Patience not for a year or two years but perhaps for as long as ten years until they could start producing star players from within their own system.

In 1977 the Blue Jays did not have enough players under contract to stock more than one team. That team was situated in Utica, New York, and played in the Class A New York-Penn League. A year later the Blue Jays had roots in four cities: Kinston, North Carolina, Dunedin, and Medicine Hat, Alberta, in Class A, and Syracuse at the AAA level. Ten years later the chain included six teams. Syracuse remained the AAA affiliate; Knoxville was at the AA level; Myrtle Beach, Dunedin, St. Catharines, Ontario, and Medicine Hat played at the A-class level. The team also maintained a team in the Dominican Republic for youngsters not quite ready to make the big cultural leap into North American society.

♦ SOW AND YE SHALL REAP

The term "farm system" provides about as clear an image as any to describe what goes on in a major-league organization. Just as a farmer spends his days coaxing crops to fruition, so the people running a baseball farm system spend their days nurturing the talent the scouting staff provides. But if this were truly a farm, then the living would be spartan indeed.

How do we know? Why, the statistics, of course. For every twenty starry-eyed players who sign a contract to play professional baseball, one will make it to the major leagues. That's about a five-percent return.

"It took us about ten years to establish a flow of players from our system," said Pat Gillick in the spring of 1988. "Along the way we had a few who came along, but now we have the ability to look for the pieces to the puzzle from our own system."

"The system" was the foundation upon which the ball club's master plan was based. And there existed a no more qualified man to see it through than Gillick, the man who has been in charge of the team's baseball operations since 1976.

It is somewhat ironic that the Blue Jays can thank George Steinbrenner's stubborn streak for the presence in their front office of one of the brightest minds in professional sports management today.

Gillick was co-ordinator of player development for Steinbrenner's New York Yankees when the Blue Jays came into being. When Toronto's interest in Gillick became apparent, Steinbrenner promised him a chance to be the Yankees' general manager "sometime in the future." Gillick asked that the promise be put in writing. Steinbrenner balked and Gillick bolted.

Pat Gillick was born August 22, 1937, in Chico, California, about one hundred miles north of the state capital in Sacramento. While Pat was still a toddler, his mother, Thelma, a one-time silent-screen actress, and his father, Larry, the local sheriff, went their separate ways. Young Patrick spent his formative years in Los Angeles, raised in large measure by his maternal grandparents.

Even though his dad didn't play a major role in his upbringing, he certainly provided the appropriate genes. Larry Gillick, who died suddenly in the fall of 1988, was a minor-league pitcher of some note, and his accurate right arm served him well as a lawman. In thirty-two years as sheriff of Butte County, Larry Gillick never once fired his gun in the line of duty. He preferred to bring down suspects by flinging rocks at them. "I thought I might hurt someone," he

Jim Clancy emerged as the ace of the Jays' pitching staff in 1978, winning ten games.

said when he retired in 1982. "I always figured I could do better with a pocketful of rocks."

♦ HOOVER LOSES TO HOUSTON

When he was nine, Pat went off to military school. During his next nine years, Gillick — whose IQ was once measured at 169, nine points above the level considered genius — developed both academic and athletic prowess. It was during this period that his now-legendary memory emerged. "It's not a matter of having a photographic memory at all," he says. "I think it has something to do with all the memorizing I had to do at school. There were a lot of rules, and we had to be able to recite them on command."

Years later, as a pitcher in the Baltimore Orioles' chain, Gillick used to floor his teammates — and Earl Weaver, his manager — with his ability to answer the most obscure baseball questions off the top of his head. Teammate Ray Yongdahl nicknamed Gillick "Wolley Segap" (Yellow Pages spelled backwards).

In September, 1963, Gillick came to a crossroads in his life. At age twenty-six, a sore left arm had finished his active career as a player. In the off-season while he had been playing, he had also been working on his master's degree. "I was thinking about law school," he recalls. "During the last couple of years of high school I had spent a lot of time with my dad, and I'd been drawn toward a career in law enforcement. Specifically the FBI. So that was sitting there on the back burner all the time I was playing."

John Mayberry was never as elegant running bases as swinging a bat.

Poised to go to work for J. Edgar Hoover, he got a phone call from Eddie Robinson, a former batting instructor who had met Gillick in the Baltimore minor-league chain. "He wanted me to be assistant farm director in the Houston chain. To be frank, I wasn't that crazy about the idea but I sat on it a couple of weeks and decided to give it a shot."

More than a quarter century later Gillick has ferreted out baseball talent from the Yucatán to the Yukon, from Moncton to Maracaibo. He's flown in a corporate jet, and he's ridden in a railway cart pulled by a donkey. "I loved the work right from the start," he says. "There is a certain amount of freedom in the game I found suited me. Maybe it's because I lived a very regimented childhood, dictated by rules and regulations. Baseball offered me the opportunity not to live by a nine-to-five schedule."

◆ A TRIPLE PLAY

The '78 Jays lived and died by their own 162-game schedule. When training camp convened in Dunedin, the prevailing sentiment was that the pitching staff would be more or less solid and would at least keep the team's record at a respectable level.

Unfortunately, that was not the case. Dave Lemanczyk, who won thirteen games in 1977, could not duplicate his previous effectiveness. He was, in fact, horrendous, finishing with a 4-14 record and a 6.26 ERA. He lost his first seven games, and by the all-star break was a pitiable 3-10. Left-handers Jerry Garvin and Tom Underwood, who had come to Toronto with reliever Victor Cruz in a deal that sent Pete Vuckovich and John Scott to St. Louis, combined to win just ten games. As noted, Cruz was one of the few pleasant surprises, along with Jim

Doug Ault will always be remembered for his two home runs on opening day in 1977, but he was also a valuable member of the team for three full seasons.

Pat Gillick, architect of the Blue Jays' subsequent successes, suffered along with the rest in 1978.

Clancy. Clancy finished with a modest total of ten wins, but that was good enough to lead the staff.

Clancy was also involved in the team's first triple play on April 22 in front of a crowd of more than 44,000 fans, including Prime Minister Pierre Trudeau. Clancy was in a spot of trouble in the second inning — none out, runners at first and second. Chicago's Junior Moore squared to bunt but popped it up to Clancy. He fired to first baseman Mayberry, doubling off Ron Blomberg. Then Mayberry threw to Luis Gomez, covering second, to complete the triple play, forcing out Lamarr Johnson.

In the midst of a forlorn season the date June 26, 1978, stands out like a beacon on a dark night. Without warning the Blue Jays exploded for a 24-10 victory over the Baltimore Orioles, setting a variety of team records that still stand.

♦ STRANGER IN A STRANGE LAND

Rick Bosetti became a Blue Jay in 1978 and was an immediate hit. He had charm, wit and an aggressive style of play that caught the public's fancy. To this day, he is the only Blue Jay in history to have maintained a winter home in Toronto. In 1978 Bosetti was Toronto's lead-off hitter, batting .249 with five homers and forty-two RBIs, earning him a spot on the Topps major-league all-rookie team.

But Bosetti was merely keeping things warm in centre field until the farm system could home-grow a star. While he was hustling all over Exhibition Stadium, a brash eighteen-year-old product of that June's draft was roaming the streets of Medicine Hat.

A stranger in a strange land, Lloyd Moseby was one frightened puppy when he arrived in Canada. Moseby was born in Arkansas but raised in Oakland, California. "I'd never been anywhere but those two places," he said. "I was scared."

But not for long. His irrepressible personality won the town over. Moseby, nicknamed "Shaker" for his ability to shed defenders on the basketball court, could often be seen on the sidewalks of Medicine Hat, passing out business cards. "Come on out to the ball park tonight and see me hit a dinger," he implored the locals. Blessed with a rare combination of physical skills — the ability to hit for power and to run the bases like a greyhound — Moseby had a ticket on the fast track to the big time. He hit .310 with ten homers and twenty steals at Medicine Hat.

Moseby was the Jays' first-round selection that year, second only to Atlanta's Bob Horner. In the fifth round they opted for another outfielder, but he did not meet with the same immediate success. By season's end that young man from Southern Illinois University was hitting only .192 in Dunedin. He hit just one homer and drove in nine runs. There was, however, still hope for the handsome twenty-one-year-old. He possessed an extraordinarily lively arm. So scout Bobby Mattick planted the seed in the young man's mind. "How about giving it a shot as a pitcher?"

Reluctantly Dave Stieb agreed.

Multitalented Lloyd Moseby was Toronto's first choice in the 1978 draft.

1979

GROWING PAINS

The hope and frustration of the Blue Jays' early years were perhaps most eloquently stated on the T-shirt worn by a fan one sunny Florida morning in March, 1979: "Toronto Blue Jays, World Series, 1985."

It required undying optimism to be a Blue Jays fan in those days, but not even the Pollyannas who hung over the fence at Dunedin that morning could have foreseen how agonizingly close that prediction would come to reality six years later.

Certainly not Bob Bailor. To survive the daily trials of being a Blue Jay in 1979, a man had to know how to deal with failure. "There have been a few times I've sounded off after a game, told everybody how tired I was of losing, but that's just the way I react to losing day after day," he told Allen Abel of *The Globe and Mail.* "Some guys laugh it off. Some guys curse. Some guys don't say anything. I always can get myself geared up the next day, shake off the loss and say, 'Let's go get 'em,' but then I'm standing out there in the outfield and it's the second inning and we're down three or four runs already, and I just think, 'Aw, geez, here we go again.' Then you find yourself behind, 14-0, and you stand there and say, 'God, hurry up and get this over with.' "

One of Pat Gillick's best trades brought shortstop Alfredo Griffin to Toronto for the 1979 season. He shared American League rookie-of-the-year honors with Minnesota's John Castino.

It was the team's worst season. The Blue Jays lost 109 games. As late as July 1, when they were already thirty-one and a half games behind the Baltimore Orioles, Toronto was on a pace to finish with the worst record in American League history. They were spared that inglorious distinction only by the pathetic Philadelphia Athletics of 1916. The As won 36 and lost 117 that year. Still, Toronto's 53-109 mark in '79 was, and is, the worst record compiled by an American League team in sixty-three years.

♦ "NATIONAL JOKE?"

As could be expected, nerves became frazzled that long frustrating summer. Hartsfield berated his players. The players, in turn, sounded off to the press about their dislike and lack of respect for Hartsfield. During a disastrous West Coast swing in August, pitcher Tom Buskey called Hartsfield "a lousy manager." Less than a week later the Jays were beaten 24-2 by the California Angels. It still stands as the most lopsided margin of defeat in the club's history.

That game ended with first baseman-designated hitter Craig Kusick on the mound. He pitched the final two and two-thirds innings. "I just wanted to throw it down the middle so nobody got hurt," said Kusick.

It was perhaps the lowest ebb in the club's history. Wrote columnist Jim Coleman, one of the most respected of all chroniclers of Canadian sport: "The Blue Jays are a national joke. Those romper-clad ingrates, masquerading as major-league baseball players, are the most overpublicized bunch of hired athletes ever to perform in a Canadian stadium."

Through it all, there remained a tiny pinprick of light at the end of the tunnel. At the heart of the ball club, away from the constant turmoil, a nucleus of exceptional talent was forming. During the previous off-season Gillick had masterminded a deal with Cleveland, sending pitcher Victor Cruz to the other side of Lake Erie in exchange for shortstop Alfredo Griffin and Phil Lansford, brother of future batting champ Carney Lansford. It was a master stroke.

Cruz would never again approach the career season he enjoyed in 1978. Though Lansford never panned out, Griffin became the embodiment of the young Blue Jays and eventually led them out of the wilderness. He shared the 1979 rookie-of-the-year honors with Minnesota's John Castino, batting .287 in the process.

Griffin remained a fixture at shortstop for Toronto for the better part of six years, playing hard, playing hurt and playing well. He became, in time, the unofficial leader in the clubhouse, universally respected for his unselfish dedication to the good of the team. Ironically, it was fellow Dominican Tony Fernandez, who grew up idolizing Griffin, who eventually forced the Jays to make a move.

Griffin accepted the inevitable with grace, and Blue Jays management packaged him up with Dave Collins and sent him to Oakland in exchange for star relief pitcher Bill Caudill at the end of 1984.

♦ A SCOUT'S DREAM COME TRUE

Griffin wasn't the only critical addition the Jays made that year.

Until his junior year at Southern Illinois University, Dave Stieb had never pitched at all. The scouting reports on his ability as an outfielder were mixed, but a strange twist of fate prevailed.

Not long before the 1978 draft, Al LaMacchia and Bobby Mattick were dispatched by Gillick to scout games in the same area. One of the games was rained out, so Gillick told both men to attend the game between Southern Illinois and Eastern Illinois. Their primary objective was to get a good reading on an outfielder named Billy Hayes, a top-fifty prospect. They'd also had reports on an outfielder named Stieb.

Nobody remembers much about Hayes, but LaMacchia and Mattick were both impressed with the guy Southern Illinois pulled out of the outfield to finish up the game on the mound. It was only the second game Stieb had ever pitched in his life. "Mattick and LaMacchia called me and told me they'd just seen this kid who'd knocked their eyes out," recalled Gillick years later.

Before they headed off for their next assignments, LaMacchia and Mattick chatted with Stieb. "They asked me if I'd pitch if I was drafted," says Stieb. "I told them I'd always been an outfielder and wanted to be one, but, sure, if I couldn't make it as an everyday player, I'd give it a try."

"I like this boy's chances on the mound," Mattick wrote in his report. "He has a good arm. Will have a good slider. Do not care for him as an outfielder."

A few weeks later the Jays drafted Stieb in the fifth round, and after signing for a bonus of $28,000, he was assigned to Dunedin to get his chance to be an outfielder. In thirty-five games he hit .195 with a homer and nine RBIs. End of experiment. Near the end of August he pitched in four games and then went on to the Instructional League in September to work on pitching technique, preparing for what most believed would be a long climb to the majors.

The inviting fences at Grant Field in Dunedin can hardly be called a pitcher's ally, but Stieb was unfazed as the 1979 season dawned. After eight starts at Dunedin, Stieb's record was 5-0 with a 4.24 ERA. Gillick and his staff had seen enough to know Stieb was wasting his time at A class. He was promoted to Syracuse. In seven starts there his record was 5-2, but his earned-run average had nose-dived to 2.13.

"Nothing ever had to be done to his delivery or mechanics," explained Gillick. "He naturally had a near-perfect release. He was one of those guys who come along once in a scout's lifetime, so natural there wasn't anything to be taught." Many pitchers spend a good deal of their professional lives trying to perfect a passable slider. Stieb's was nasty right from the beginning.

Years later, when he ran into trouble, Stieb looked back on his conversion to pitching with some amazement. "It boggles me now, especially after what I've been through, that ability I had to throw the slider. I could just push a button and here comes a slider on the black."

◆ ONE OF THE BEST

On June 29, 1979, Dave Stieb made his major-league debut against the eventual pennant-winning Baltimore Orioles. It was not pretty. He was touched up for two home runs — the first he'd ever allowed as a professional — as the Os rolled up a 6-1 score. But it was not a sign of things to come.

While the Jays continued to wallow, Stieb was clearly a cut above. He finished that season 8-8 at the major-league level, a thoroughly astonishing accomplishment for one who had pitched his first games only a year before. A year later his name was being discussed in the same breath with some of the best pitchers in baseball.

He also developed a brash, swaggering public persona. Some called it confidence. Others called it arrogance. A teammate's error was treated with an icy

Top: *Vancouver-born second baseman Dave McKay was a rarity in baseball: a major-leaguer from Canada.*

Bottom: *After two solid seasons, Bob Bailor slumped in 1979.*

Right: *Dave Stieb was signed as an outfielder after the 1978 draft but his meteoric rise to the majors came after he began concentrating on pitching.*

BLUE JAYS

stare or a gesture of disgust; an opponent's base hit was treated with the same disdain.

It was a phase of his career Stieb would outgrow. One day in 1985, a more mature Stieb tried to put it in perspective. "To begin with," he explained, "remember that I'd never been a pitcher and never had to deal with depending upon somebody else. If I made an error in centre field, it was my error and hurt somebody else. As a pitcher you're dependent on others, and I had to learn to deal with that."

He won twelve games in 1980, eleven in '81 then seventeen in '82 and '83. In '84 he won sixteen games and followed that with fourteen in the '85 championship season, the same year he signed a multiyear, multimillion-dollar contract that gave him security for life.

But when '86 dawned, Stieb was suddenly mortal. The crackling slider was hittable. The fastball on the corner was just a fraction of an inch outside. The runs piled up, and so did the losses. He was 0-6 when he went to the mound on May 30, finally getting his first win of the year almost two months into the season. But that wasn't the end of it. By the all-star break in mid-July he was 2-9 with a whopping 5.80 ERA. It was a stunning blow to one so naturally gifted. Ironically, it may have been that gift that prevented him from overcoming the problems.

"Dave had never struggled," said pitching coach Al Widmar. "He had never had to deal with adversity. Pitching is composed of a lot of bits and pieces. Talent is obviously the most important thing. But it's not the only thing. A lot of what makes a great pitcher is learned. Dave never had an opportunity to learn."

Stieb finished 1986 with a bit of a flourish, winning three of his last five decisions in September to finish at 7-12 for the season. But he was still not nearly the same pitcher he'd been before. There was the matter of a bone spur that had caused pain in his pitching elbow.

"For me to go nine [innings] used to be no trouble," he told Steve Milton of *The Hamilton Spectator* early in 1988. "But last year and the year before, when I was struggling, I would think about the game I was going to pitch and say, 'There's no way I'm going to go nine.' It seemed like such a feat. Right there I didn't have the right attitude; I'm almost beat. So I've started thinking about one hitter, then the next — pretty soon you're in the ninth inning."

Stieb's new maturity paid off in his best season of the last three in 1988. He finished with seventeen wins, but he really caught everyone's attention with his last two incredible starts of 1988, missing no-hitters in each by just one pitch.

♦ TIME FOR CHANGE

But in the middle of 1979 Dave Stieb was just another rookie on a struggling pitching staff. Jim Clancy, impressive in 1978, missed much of the year with ankle problems. Dave Lemanczyk bounced back from a poor 1978 to be at least respectable. But the pitching staff's quality can best be judged from the fact that

John Mayberry is a heavy load for anyone but especially one so slender as Seattle's Bobby Valentine.

Tom Underwood was named the team's pitcher of the year even though he lost his first nine decisions of the season.

Offensively, big John Mayberry hit .274 with twenty-one homers and seventy-four RBIs to provide what little spark the Jays had. Rick Cerone took over as catcher after Alan Ashby was traded to Houston and provided solid defence plus sixty-one RBIs. Roy Howell was again steady, belting fifteen homers and seventy-two RBIs. On the whole, however, it was not a pretty sight. Danny Ainge, the Brigham Young basketball star, struggled on the infield, batting just .237 with two homers and nineteen RBIs. He would eventually abandon baseball for the Boston Celtics of the National Basketball Association.

When the dust had cleared from the 1979 season, it was time for some changes, starting with the manager. Hartsfield was fired, along with his coaching staff. His replacement was a sixty-three-year-old managerial rookie named Bobby Mattick, who had been responsible for signing many players in the minor system at that time. His role for the next two years was to integrate those young players into the big-league roster. It was sink or swim for the young Blue Jays.

1980

A NEW ERA

A decade that gave us Watergate, Joe Clark, the Jonestown massacre, Kent State, designer jeans, Archie Bunker, the greenhouse effect, leisure suits, Coneheads, letter bombs, Louise Brown, ultra suede, disco, jogging shoes, OPEC, "What's happenin'?," R2D2, Nadia Comaneci, the War Measures Act, Patty Hearst and, yes, the Toronto Blue Jays was at an end. Three seasons had come and gone for the Jays at the dawn of the 1980s. Like the seventies themselves, there was much to be remembered and much that deserved to be dropped like a stone into the deep, dark lake of amnesia.

The team brought an inglorious 166-318 won-lost record into the 1980 season, but few other vestiges of their dismal beginnings remained. Most of the original journeymen who had served simply as warm bodies to fill uniforms had departed.

During the off-season Pat Gillick had been busy. In addition to orchestrating the managerial and coaching transition, he had engineered some bold player moves. Rick Cerone, outfielder Ted Wilborn and pitcher Tom Underwood had been dealt to the Yankees in exchange for veteran slugger Chris Chambliss, left-handed pitcher Paul Mirabella and a minor-league infielder named Damaso Garcia. Chambliss was a reluctant Blue Jay for only thirty-four days before he was passed on to the Atlanta Braves along with shortstop Luis Gomez in exchange for outfielder Barry Bonnell, infielder Pat Rockett and pitcher Joey McLaughlin.

After a minor-league apprenticeship of two years, Lloyd Moseby joined a nucleus of young talented players giving the team fresh hope for the future.

In place now was the core of talent that would eventually develop, allowing the team to become a strong contender in the tough American League East Division: Dave Stieb. Jim Clancy. Luis Leal. Damaso Garcia. Barry Bonnell. Alfredo Griffin. Garth Iorg. Lloyd Moseby. Ernie Whitt.

Some of the old mainstays were still around, steadying influences for the new wave: Dave Lemanczyk, Jesse Jefferson, Doug Ault, Otto Velez, John Mayberry,

Left: *Rick Bosetti hit only four home runs in 1980 but this one beat the Brewers 1-0 in the bottom of the ninth inning on April 17. Here, Bosetti gets a hug from winning pitcher Paul Mirabella.*

Right: *At the age of sixty-three, Bobby Mattick became the game's oldest rookie.*

Roy Howell and Bob Bailor. But for most of them this season would be their last in a Blue Jays uniform.

Bobby Mattick, who had nurtured many of the baby Jays through their minor-league apprenticeships, was now the club manager — "the oldest rookie [at sixty-three] ever in the big leagues," he chirped. He brought along a new staff that included a hardworking third-base coach named Jimy Williams.

♦ UNBRIDLED OPTIMISM

Despite the black cloud of a potential players' strike that hung over the proceedings from the very beginning of spring training, and despite a short holdout by Dave Stieb, there was a fresh attitude in the Blue Jays' clubhouse. For the first time in its short history the team won more games than it lost during the strike-abbreviated Grapefruit League season in Florida, taking ten of seventeen games.

When the players' association decided to start the season and continue to negotiate a new collective bargaining agreement, Toronto's newly discovered enthusiasm carried it through the early part of the schedule, retaining at least a share of first place as late as May 10 as they won fifteen of their first twenty-five games.

There was unbridled optimism in Toronto. For the first time the Jays appeared on NBC's game of the week. Their progress was noted in prominently displayed feature stories in newspapers across the United States. A naively euphoric atmosphere prevailed. It was still only May, with nearly five months of baseball remaining to be played.

"Their biggest enemy," wrote Thomas Boswell in *The Washington Post*, "is not their modest talent or their manager's inexperience or even their own dismal history. It is their current unrealistic excess of happiness and the swarms of soft-headed folk who are wishing them well in the pennant race."

A strike deadline had been set, but a shut-down was averted by a last-minute settlement in the wee hours of May 23. The main issue — free-agent compensation — would eventually lead to a prolonged strike in 1981, but for the moment the sombre mood had lifted. "I felt if it came to a strike," said Peter Bavasi, "we would lose something more important than money, something we could not recover — namely, the tremendous spirit and confidence the players on this team have developed."

Of course, the pennant race was some distance over the horizon. Slowly the Jays drifted lower. When the sun came up on June 1, they were above .500 for the last time that season, having won twenty-two of forty-three games, good enough for third place, five and a half games back of the Yankees. They were again on their way to last place, but they weren't going quietly.

Pitching was the team's strong point. By mid-June they had clipped a full run from their team earned-run average (4.82 to 3.82). Beyond that, the Jays had won four games by the score of 1-0, and that was four more than they had accomplished in their three previous seasons. "Everybody knows now that after you get past Stieb, you still have to face Clancy, Mirabella and Leal," pointed out pitching coach Al Widmar proudly.

Despite the improvement on defence, by June 17 they were back on familiar ground: seventh place, ten games out. The team again finished last, but for the first time they lost fewer than one hundred games. Their overall record of 67-95 was perceived as a major breakthrough, a warning to the rest of baseball that very shortly the Jays would be a force to be reckoned with.

◆ ERRRRR-NIE! ERRRRR-NIE!

The trading of Cerone was a clear signal that Whitt would be the team's number-one catcher, a quantum leap of confidence from that shown him by previous manager Hartsfield.

Going back as far as 1977, Hartsfield and Whitt had been at odds. "That first spring," Whitt recalls, "I went in to say something to [Hartsfield] who took offence at what I said and he held it against me."

During the spring of 1979, after a spring training game in which Whitt had twice cut down Lou Brock, the all-time major-league base thief, Hartsfield called Whitt into his office. "He said, 'Son, you just don't have the arm to throw anyone out. You can't play in the big leagues for me.' I looked at Roy and said, 'What are you looking at? Something is obviously wrong.' "

Whitt went back to Syracuse, where he won the Sporting News Silver Glove award for superior defence and in the process helped the Chiefs get to the International League finals.

When Mattick took over as manager, one of his first moves was to install Whitt

JAYS

For nine consecutive seasons, beginning in 1980 and ending in 1988, pitcher Jim Clancy (left) *and catcher Ernie Whitt* (above) *proved a formidable combination.*

as his number-one catcher, allowing Gillick to trade Rick Cerone. It was the beginning of a long and mutually rewarding relationship between Whitt and the city of Toronto.

Way down deep, if Ernie Whitt had had his druthers, he would have been a Detroit Tiger. Born not six blocks from Tiger Stadium, he grew up in the suburb of Roseville, his world dominated by sports. When he wasn't playing baseball or football or perhaps fighting with one of the neighborhood kids, Ernie would arrive at Tiger Stadium early to situate himself strategically in the right-field seats and chase down the majestic batting-practice homers stroked by Al Kaline and Norm Cash, the Tiger heroes of the day.

Ernie became a catcher by default at the age of six. There was one spot left on the team and that was behind the plate. Even from that early age he attacked his dream of being a big-leaguer with relentless determination.

It was not the only thing he attacked. "I was a real tough guy in the fifth grade," he says. "I was always fighting, trying to see who was the toughest guy around. It was the thing to do."

Whitt's dream of playing with the Tigers never materialized. Though he was a big local star as a teenager, the Detroit club felt he would never be any better than a AA catcher. The Red Sox, however, took a shot, signing him in 1972.

After four years of kicking around the Red Sox system, Whitt was invited to the big leagues for a September look-see in 1976. In his first major-league at-bat he connected for a home run against Milwaukee's Jim Colborn. But it was his first starting assignment that he remembers best. "We were in Tiger Stadium, and Carlton Fisk [the regular Boston catcher] came up to me on the Friday night and said, 'You're from this area, aren't you?' When I told him I was, he said, 'Get your rest tonight because you're catching tomorrow.' I came to the park the next day and [manager] Don Zimmer said, 'Fisk isn't feeling well. You're starting.' It was a huge thrill."

But there was really no future for Whitt in Boston. Fisk, at twenty-eight, was a fixture at Fenway Park. And Whitt wasn't getting any younger. He was already twenty-four, with still no light at the end of the tunnel.

Then, on November 5, 1976, it all changed. That was the day of the expansion draft, and Whitt was the seventeenth player selected by the Blue Jays.

No player who ever played for the Jays has been responsible for putting more back into the community. His annual golf tournament regularly raises $25,000 for the Kidney Foundation of Canada, and a couple of years ago he was the honorary chairman of the Canadian Cancer Society.

He is occasionally needled by his teammates because of his popularity in Canada. One of his clubhouse nicknames is "Mr. Prime Minister." One day during June, 1988, at a time when a half-dozen of the world's most powerful political leaders converged on Toronto for a week-long conference, Whitt was a few minutes late getting to the park. When he arrived, one of his teammates looked at his watch and said, "The Summit must be over. Ernie's here."

Beyond that, he has been a solid, dependable performer with a penchant for delivering in the crunch. In his last seven seasons with the Jays he has averaged fifteen homers and sixty RBIs to go with a solid .255 batting average. Try comparing those numbers with most other catchers in baseball, and you'll probably find Whitt in the top five.

◆ THE DOUGHNUT KING

Whitt is also among the top five pranksters in Blue Jays history, always ready to liven things up when he feels the mood needs it. That also makes him a prime target.

As a prodigious consumer of doughnuts and one who must carefully monitor his weight, he is often ribbed about this obvious conflict. He recalls one incident in Oakland in 1985 in particular: "I laid down a bunt that day and was thrown out by a fair bit. A few batters later, a batting doughnut came off the end of a bat and rolled near our dugout. Bobby Cox said, 'Quick, someone get that before Ernie eats it.' Well, things built from there. We went out on the field and came back for our next at-bats. As I was getting ready, I found someone had fixed a wire from the top of my batting helmet. A doughnut hung from one end in front of the helmet, like a carrot for a donkey."

But in 1980 Whitt was just one of a dozen struggling young players trying to make an impression. And, in many cases, succeeding.

The double-play combination of shortstop Alfredo Griffin and second baseman Damaso Garcia was akin to ballet in baseball cleats. They were the main reasons that the Blue Jays set an American League record for double plays — 206 — in a single season.

Lloyd Moseby, summoned to the Jays from Syracuse in late May, made an immediate impression, hitting nine homers and driving in forty-six runs. And Garth Iorg, given his first opportunity, proved himself a utility man par excellence, playing every position except catcher and pitcher. Clancy won thirteen games, Stieb an even dozen.

Perhaps spurred on by the youthful enthusiasm all around them, some of the veterans responded with big years themselves. Al Woods, bolstered by Mattick's vote of confidence, responded with a .300 batting average and fifteen homers, the best season of his career. Otto Velez hit twenty homers, including four in one memorable day at Exhibition Stadium during a doubleheader on May 4 against Cleveland. Otto the Swatto hit three homers in the first game, including a grand slam, then smacked another in the second game to account for ten RBIs during the day.

But the big bopper for Toronto in 1980 was John Mayberry, who belted thirty homers and drove in eighty-two runs, both team records at the time. The home-run record did not fall until 1986 when both George Bell and Jesse Barfield broke it.

The Jays and their fans, buoyed by the promise of 1980, eagerly awaited spring training, 1981 and another step along the road to contention. Unfortunately, no one could have predicted that step would be in the wrong direction.

BLUE JAYS

1981

LOSERS, ALL

The year 1981 represented an unsightly stain on baseball's tapestry. If this was a book of baseball's best moments, undoubtedly there would be several blank pages where the chronicles of such a blighted season should have been. For two years the owners and players had been heading for an inevitable confrontation. When it finally came, the strike caused the most dismal two months in the grand old game's history.

The collision between management and players over the complicated issue of free agency compensation was somehow avoided until June 12, when the players did not report for work. For the next fifty-nine days ball parks all over North America were dark and silent, mute reminders that for all its presumed innocence, for all its romantic lore, baseball is big business.

Perhaps Ken Griffey, then a star outfielder with the Cincinnati Reds, best described the sense of depression that pervaded throughout the summer. "Everyone is losing in this strike," he said, "whether it's the fans, the players, the owners and even the nation as a whole. When you get right down to it, the really sad thing is that no one is winning."

Ironically, the strike may have been a good thing for the Blue Jays. Since the team had come off such a promising year in 1980, most observers expected the Jays to take another step forward down the road to contention. But there is no denying that when the strike arrived the Blue Jays were in a sorry state. They had won just sixteen of their first fifty-eight games. Projected over an entire season, their .276 winning percentage would have produced 117 losses, eight more than the disastrous 1979 season.

Like most of the Blue Jays, Damaso Garcia had a disappointing season in 1981 but he was a key for the future.

As the shut-down began, they were in the throes of an eleven-game losing streak that would eventually become an even dozen — the longest in team history. As a team they were hitting a miserable .218. On June 11, the last day of play, frustrated fans chanted "Strike! Strike! Strike!" during Kansas City's easy 10-5 win over Toronto.

During the strike, ticket seller Al Ross had the loneliest job in town.

"It's a chance to get away from the rut we've been in," said Dave Stieb. "It seems like the more we've tried, the more everything has been going against us. This has been a very discouraging season, particularly after last year when we seemed to be making progress."

The season was a particularly galling one for Mattick, who once described himself as "patient, but I'm a bit short-fused if I see that players aren't giving their best effort." When Mattick signed on as manager at the start of the 1980 season, he was sixty-three and had not worn a uniform since 1948. During the course of those thirty years he had become a legend among his peers, working in player development and as a scout for a half-dozen teams.

The list of players he scouted and signed is a veritable who's who of baseball: Frank Robinson, Vada Pinson, Curt Flood, Jim Maloney and Tommy Harper during his years with Cincinnati. For Houston, he tabbed Rusty Staub and Dave Giusti. At Seattle and Milwaukee, he picked Darrell Porter, Gorman Thomas and Sixto Lezcano. As a Baltimore scout, he delivered Bobby Grich and Don Baylor. To the Expos, he sent Gary Carter, Warren Cromartie, Ellis Valentine and Gary Roenicke.

Mattick's dad, Chick, had been a major-leaguer, and Bobby, a sure-handed shortstop, had similar aspirations. But a freak accident — a foul ball that hit him while he waited in the on-deck circle while playing in Los Angeles in 1936 — caused vision problems that never healed.

After two weeks in hospital Mattick was back at the ball park, doggedly trying

The 1981 season was a frustrating one for manager Bobby Mattick.

to play with double vision. Six years later the frustration of trying to hit a baseball when he saw two coming at him compelled him to quit. That's when he embarked on his true calling.

When his sentence as Blue Jays manager was up at the end of '81, again he went back to what he loved best — developing talent in the Blue Jays' system.

♦ JEKYLL AND HYDE

Years later, to look back at the prestrike Blue Jays and compare them to the post-strike Blue Jays is to look at the records of two entirely different teams. During the so-called "second-season" the Jays put together a creditable 21-27 record and appeared to have put their early-season woes behind them.

In a much larger context the strike represents a dividing line between the expansion Jays and the contending Jays. In four and a half seasons before the strike, Toronto's record was 249-455, a winning percentage of just .354. In the next seven and a half years the team won 644 and lost 537, a winning percentage of .545, which ranks among the best in baseball.

But none of this was self-evident during the angry summer of 1981. The Blue Jay offence, which left Florida full of confidence because of a lusty .305 spring training batting average, was terrible. The evening of May 15 in Cleveland was perhaps indicative. On that night Len Barker pitched the first American League perfect game in thirteen years, blanking the Jays 3-0.

That was just one of twenty shutout defeats the Jays suffered that season.

Left: *George Bell turned out to be a steal in the major-league draft. Taken from Philadelphia in 1980, Bell eventually became the league's most valuable player.*

Right: *During his six seasons with the Blue Jays, second baseman Damaso Garcia earned a reputation as one of the most elegant pivotmen in the game.*

Damaso Garcia was the only regular to hit better than .250, but just barely. He hit .252. The team finished with a .226 team batting average, scoring just 329 runs in 106 games. John Mayberry, in what would be his last full season with Toronto, provided a shred of respectability by hitting seventeen homers and driving in forty-three runs in ninety-four games.

All that saved the Jays from complete embarrassment was a pitching staff that improved significantly in its earned-run average and in walks surrendered.

Officially the strike ended on Friday, July 31. A short training period led up to the resumption of play on August 10. The Jays picked up right where they left off, losing 4-3 in ten innings at Detroit. But from there they went on a mini-spurt, winning seven of their next ten.

Late in August, it became apparent that Danny Ainge would soon be leaving the club to play professional basketball in Boston. For the second straight year he hit under .200 while generating little or no power.

When the books were closed on Toronto's fifth consecutive last-place finish, the winds of change had already reached gale force in the Blue Jays' executive offices. Several members of the management team, including Paul Beeston and Pat Gillick, were on the verge of quitting. Beeston, in fact, had already tendered his resignation. At the core of the unrest was Bavasi's insufferable personality.

Now that the Jays were on the verge of becoming a championship contender, it was agreed that a new, dynamic manager must be located. Mattick's role as teacher-counsellor was done. Gillick settled on former Atlanta manager Bobby Cox as the best available man, but he had a difficult job convincing Bavasi to hire him. Eventually Bavasi relented, and on October 15, Cox became the team's third manager.

That autumn, after studying the situation in the baseball team's front office, chief executive officer Peter Hardy suggested to Bavasi that it was perhaps time he moved on. Bavasi was not fired, but the message was perfectly clear.

♦ THE THRILL IS GONE

On November 24, four years from the day he had been promoted to team president, Bavasi announced his resignation to a jammed news conference at the Sheraton Centre. In his farewell he said, "The thrill of building the Blue Jays is gone. Now patient maintenance is needed. I haven't got a lot of patience maintaining things. I've seen the picture before. It's like going to a movie like *Gone With The Wind* four or five times. It's a great movie but after a while you want to see *Ben-Hur*."

Later, speaking with Allen Abel of *The Globe and Mail*, he said, "I left because of illness. They were sick of me and I was sick of them."

That may well have been true. But there is no denying that Bavasi was the driving force behind the team's early box office success.

Five years after their birth the Toronto Blue Jays had become, undisputedly, the most successful expansion franchise in baseball history, at least financially.

And the best was still to come. There existed the sense that 1981 was just a

Peter Bavasi said his goodbyes at a press conference on November 24, 1981.

momentary setback. The young talent was still in place. Alfredo Griffin had had a bad season, but he would bounce back. Through shrewd use of the major-league draft, Gillick had pilfered a young Dominican slugger named George Bell from the Philadelphia Phillies organization. Dave Stieb had managed to win eleven games, averaging better than seven innings in each of his twenty-five starts.

On September 3, in the opener of a four-game series at Comiskey Park in Chicago, Bobby Mattick filled in a lineup card that included for the first time the names Bell, Moseby and Barfield in the Blue Jays outfield. Born within two weeks of one another, Bell in the Dominican Republic, Moseby in Arkansas and Barfield in Illinois, there was no telling what the future might hold for this trio.

Meanwhile, in a dusty little North Carolina town named Kinston, a nineteen-year-old prodigy was honing his breathtaking skills on the lumpy infield of Grainger Stadium. "He has the best instincts of any prospect I've ever seen," said Kinston manager John McLaren, now the Jays' third-base coach. "He can read a ground ball better than any minor-leaguer I've ever seen, even on this infield."

Already Tony Fernandez was getting rave reviews.

1982

A NEW ATTITUDE

There was never a magic wand. No mysterious elixir. But clearly there was a different mood around Dunedin in 1982 when the Blue Jays came south to roost in February. "For a lot of us who had been around through the bad times, it was becoming clear that we were finally headed somewhere," said catcher Ernie Whitt. "And everyone had faith that Bobby Cox was the guy who would be able to take us there."

Roy Hartsfield and Bobby Mattick had been caretaker managers, men who could take the team through the early phases of their development. Now Cox had been hired, a signal to the players and to the public that things were getting serious. "A lot of the groundwork has been laid here by the people who came before me," said Cox that spring. "I guess it's my job to try to get us over the top, but really all I'll be doing is an extension of what Roy and Bobby did ahead of me."

Robert Joe Cox was born May 21, 1941, in Tulsa, Oklahoma, but grew up in Selma, California, a farming community fifteen miles south of Fresno, near the midpoint between Los Angeles and San Francisco.

"From as far back as I can remember, we played ball," he says. "I mean morning, noon and night. I couldn't get enough of it. Still can't."

People who saw him play through eight minor-league seasons and two in the majors remember him not for his talent but for his hustle and determination. He was the kind of guy who would chase a pop foul one hundred feet down the line, knowing it was probably in the seats. "He was an average major-leaguer with a lot of enthusiasm," said the late Dick Howser, who played with Cox in New York. "The type of guy who enjoyed putting on the uniform. I know for a fact that as often as not he was hurting pretty bad, but you practically had to hog-tie him to get him out of a game."

With the arrival of Bobby Cox as manager at the start of the 1982 season, the Blue Jays were poised to take flight.

Cox was one of the original bonus babies, that first wave of players who were

offered eye-popping financial incentives to sign. He received $40,000 from the Los Angeles Dodgers to sign in 1959, spending seven years in the Dodger chain, another year with the Braves and then two in the big leagues with the Yankees as their third baseman in 1969-70.

"But my knees were gone. Blown out. I couldn't play anymore," he says. "I couldn't make the Yankee club in 1971." That year he played in Syracuse, but a year later he was managing in Fort Lauderdale for the Yankees. His team was composed of young players, most of them in their teens. "I tell you I wouldn't trade those days for anything in the world. I had more damn fun. My philosophy was that every one of those damn kids was going to become a major-leaguer."

♦ A BOND OF TRUST

Cox moved up the chain until he became a coach under Billy Martin in 1977. A year later he landed the managing job in Atlanta, where he found himself in the middle of a rebuilding program. Just when it was nearly complete, he was reluctantly fired by owner Ted Turner. Pat Gillick, a friend, immediately realized Cox would be perfect for the Toronto job.

The new manager quickly forged a bond of trust and respect with the young Blue Jays players. He was honest, sincere and unfailingly loyal. Early he made it clear he wasn't in the game to satisfy his own ego. "I'd just as soon never see my name in print," he said. And when he said something, he meant it.

"Bobby never asked much of a player except to give a good honest effort," said Rance Mulliniks. "Give him one hundred percent, and he sticks by you through thick and thin."

"Tough, but not overbearing," was Willie Upshaw's assessment. "Play hard, play smart, and then it's time to relax. He knows you're going to have bad days and good days. One bad day is not going to make you or break you in his eyes."

A significant feature of the Cox regime was the strict platoon system he

Left: *Buck Martinez brought the young Jays his ten years of catching experience.*

Right: *Willie Upshaw unseated John Mayberry as the starting first baseman in the spring of 1982.*

employed to get the most out of certain players. Ernie Whitt and Buck Martinez became the catching tandem, Whitt facing all right-handed pitchers, Martinez playing against lefties. Rance Mulliniks and Garth Iorg did the same at third base, Mulliniks against righties, Iorg against left-handers. And in the outfield Jesse Barfield shared right field with Hosken Powell. Later, in 1984, Barfield and Dave Collins platooned.

"Ernie was never better," said Martinez, looking back at 1982, "I was never better. Rance and Garth had never been better. And everybody in the park knew Barfield was going to be an everyday player. Coxie just patiently brought him along. I've seen young players ruined by putting them in over their heads too early."

Largely as a result of the rigid platoon, the Blue Jays tied the American League record for pinch hits with seventy-one, accounting for fifty-three RBIs, more than double the average of the rest of the league.

♦ RESPECTABLE AT LAST

After a strong showing in spring training, the team did not get off to a big start. By the end of April they had won just eight of twenty games. Willie Upshaw had

taken John Mayberry's job at first base during spring training, and to show the move was permanent, Mayberry was traded to the Yankees on May 5 in exchange for Dave Revering.

On that day they lost their fifteenth game in twenty-four starts. From that point forward, Toronto played exactly .500 baseball through the rest of the season.

Damaso Garcia and Dave Stieb, both of whom were vocal in their criticism of management's tight fiscal policies at the time, took their arguments out to the field, where both enjoyed superior seasons. Garcia batted .310 — sixth in the league — and stole fifty-four bases, second only to Rickey Henderson's all-time record of 130. Stieb won seventeen games with a 3.25 earned-run average, leading the league with nineteen complete games and 288 innings pitched. During the second half of the season Stieb's record was 10-4 with a skimpy 2.25 ERA. Had he been pitching for a contender, Stieb probably would have won the Cy Young award that went to Milwaukee's Pete Vuckovich, a former Jay.

Jim Clancy, with sixteen wins and 267 innings, and Luis Leal, with twelve wins and 250 innings, gave Toronto three quality starters for the first time. The bull pen was somewhat shaky, but still improved. Dale Murray set a modest club record of eleven saves with Joey McLaughlin and Roy Lee Jackson adding fourteen more between them.

Murray's greatest contribution to the future of the Blue Jays did not come until after the season. That's when he was dealt to the Yankees in exchange for Dave Collins, pitcher Mike Morgan and a throw-in, a gangly first baseman from Tampa named Fred McGriff.

Alfredo Griffin made dramatic improvements on both offence and defence. In the strike-shortened '81 season he had committed an unpardonable thirty-one errors in just 101 games. In 1982 he made twenty-six miscues while playing in every one of the Jays' 162 games. Moreover, he erred just eight times in the second half of the schedule.

In addition, Griffin improved his batting average to .241 and drove in a career-high forty-eight runs and developed, by his attitude and work habits, a leadership role in the clubhouse.

On the afternoon of September 28, Stieb and the Jays defeated the Seattle Mariners 6-2 at the KingDome to complete their most successful road season at thirty-four wins and forty-seven losses.

Rance Mulliniks' career took a decided turn for the better when he was traded to Toronto from Kansas City just before the 1982 season.

♦ NEARLY PERFECT

That night the team held its annual team party in Seattle. Early the next morning they arrived at the Seattle-Tacoma Airport, which was blanketed in fog so thick they could not see the airplane waiting just outside the departure lounge window. The delays mounted up and so did the bar bill. By the time the entourage made it home late that night, a good time had been had by all, including Jim Clancy, the starting pitcher in the first game of a doubleheader the following night against Minnesota to kick off a season-ending home stand.

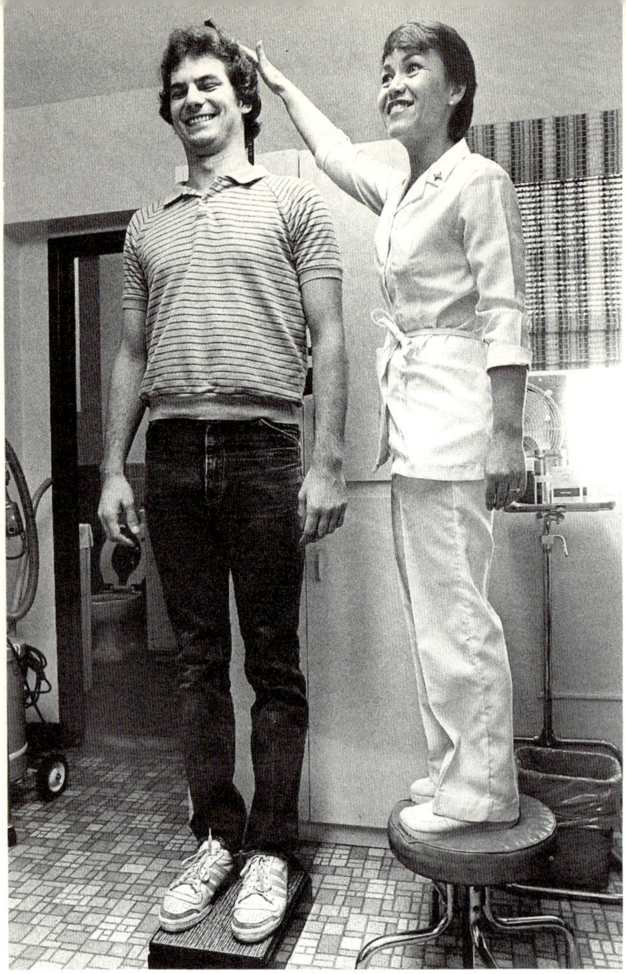

Jim Clancy's 1982 season began with medicals in Dunedin and finished with a near-miss of a no-hitter in September. He is shown here with nurse Joanne Heywood.

All Clancy did against the Twins was come achingly close to perfection. He set down the Minnesota lineup in order through eight innings. Twenty-four up and twenty-four down. No pitcher in baseball had pitched a perfect game since Len Barker had done it to the Jays a year previous. And no Blue Jay had ever pitched a no-hitter.

Part way through the game, Blue Jays CEO Peter Hardy informed Paul Beeston that if Clancy made history, he was to get an immediate $10,000 bonus and that everyone on the field would get $1,000.

"But that's about $35,000," said Beeston with a gasp.

"More like $50,000," said Hardy. "I mean *everybody* in uniform, right down to the ball boys."

But that big pay day never materialized. Minnesota designated hitter Randy Bush broke his bat and Clancy's heart leading off the ninth. The bat splintered into a dozen pieces and the ball barely eluded Garcia's outstretched glove behind second base, settling to earth as the only Minnesota hit of the game.

The hit was only slightly less heartbreaking for Clancy's teammates. Over the course of the team's history no other player was more appreciated inside the Blue Jays' clubhouse than Jim Clancy. "Clance is a player's player," says battery-mate Ernie Whitt. "He doesn't say much, he doesn't complain, ever. He just wants the ball every time it's his turn. He doesn't have an enemy in the world."

Clancy grew up in a Chicago suburb called Mount Greenwood, a strapping youngster who excelled at both football and baseball. Drafted by the Texas

Rangers out of St. Rita's High School, he was a struggling minor-leaguer with three professional seasons under his belt when the Blue Jays were awarded their franchise in the spring of 1976.

He had played at San Antonio in the AA Texas League in '76, and his numbers were unimpressive. Six wins, eight losses. A whopping 6.48 ERA. And he was wild. Ninety-eight walks and ten wild pitches in 125 innings. But Bob Miller, who would be the Jays' pitching coach, was managing at Amarillo that year and saw in Clancy a young pitcher with a great arm.

Before the Jays drafted him, Clancy was not optimistic about his big-league chances, but when he was taken in the draft, his spirits soared. "I knew then I'd have a chance to pitch in the majors," he said, "But I never imagined I'd be here for ten years." Since then he has seen it all, the good times and the bad. He has not changed one bit. He still has the easiest smile in baseball, and when he's on top of his game, he's still one of the toughest pitchers to face.

Through the Blue Jays' growing years Clancy was one of the few players a manager could count on. It was therefore sadly ironic that, in 1985, when the team finally achieved success, Clancy did not play a major role. In training camp that year he had been stricken by appendicitis. Later he had a bout of tendinitis, and when that was finished, he was ignored by manager Cox during the playoffs until he was summoned for unfamiliar relief duty in Kansas City. He is still stung by that memory. "I had hoped to get a start," he remembers. "But I don't think it was my position to be out there in a relief role, not when we had experienced relievers like [Tom] Henke or [Bill] Caudill or [Jim] Acker out there."

That is as close to a complaint as you'll ever hear from Jim Clancy. But on that night at the tail end of 1982 at Exhibition Stadium, Clancy wasn't complaining about anything.

At the end of 1988 Clancy left the Blue Jays for the Houston Astros, lured away by the prospect of a three-year contract worth $3.45 million, leaving Ernie Whitt as the only remaining original player.

♦ GOING HOME PROUD

Clancy's gem was part of a late-season spurt that allowed the Jays to avoid sole possession of the basement for the first time in their history. With seven wins in their last eight games, including a season-ending sweep of the Seattle Mariners at Exhibition Stadium, the Jays finished at 78-84, by far their best record ever and good enough for a sixth-place tie with Cleveland.

On the final day of the season, after beating Seattle for their fourth win in a row, the Blue Jays were already anticipating spring training, some five months in the future. "I can go home proud of myself for being a Toronto Blue Jay this year," said Garcia. "We made the other teams play hard to beat us. We've got guys who are going to produce — Lloyd Moseby and Jesse Barfield — and if we get that, we're going to be a contender."

"This is a competitive ball club," said Martinez. "We proved we can play with anyone. And there'll be more fun next year."

2

1983

GREAT EXPECTATIONS

Alfredo Griffin's days as the Blue Jays' shortstop would soon be cut short by the arrival of future superstar Tony Fernandez.

There is a time in all of our lives when we outgrow the sweet innocence of childhood. So it is with baseball teams, and by the summer of 1983 the Blue Jays had reached that critical moment. Nurtured by Pat Gillick's knowing hand and an adoring public, the Jays had been the golden-haired children of Toronto's sports community. Now, in 1983, after six years that benign indulgence was replaced by a strange and powerful element: hope.

And with these tiny strands of hope was spun the inevitable web of rising expectations. Forgiveness would be granted rather more grudgingly in the future for these descendants of that pioneering group of lovable bunglers. The nucleus of players that would eventually vault the team to the top of the American League East was no longer a collection of raw, untested talent. In just one year under Cox the team had begun to believe in itself.

The Jays had built a team based on speed, pitching and overall defence, and in 1983 they used all those elements to throw a huge scare into the rest of the Eastern Division.

After he'd watched his team for a few weeks in Dunedin, Cox realized something that took a few more months to become apparent to the rest of baseball: the Blue Jays had arrived. "We're gonna be tough to beat," he said. "I just hope we can sneak up on a few teams and slip by 'em when they're not paying attention."

But baseball was paying attention. You can be sure of that. Upshaw, Moseby, Stieb and Garcia were not exactly household names across the United States, but the thought of playing against them kept more than one opposition manager from sleeping at night.

"What I love about Toronto," said Tigers manager Sparky Anderson, "is that they don't even know yet how good they are. You just never know who's gonna

Overleaf, page 68: *Willie Upshaw had his best year as a Blue Jay in 1983, hitting .306 with 27 homers and 104 RBIs.*

Overleaf, page 69: *Like his good friend Upshaw, Lloyd Moseby emerged in 1983, hitting .315 with 18 homers and 81 RBIs.*

Franklin

LUEJAY

beat you. They're hungry . . . hungry for respect and hungry for a championship. I'm afraid it's just a matter of time before they satisfy that appetite."

♦ THE ODD COUPLE

Perhaps no two players personified that attitude more than Willie Upshaw and Lloyd Moseby. Both had joined the Blue Jays organization in 1978 — Moseby came through the amateur draft, and Upshaw was stolen from the Yankees in the major-league draft.

As so often seems to happen, these two oddly matched personalities became fast friends. Moseby, born in Portland, Arkansas, and raised in Oakland, California, is a bubbly, outgoing sort, always chattering. He has a flamboyant character with a wardrobe to match. Upshaw, on the other hand, is a quiet, thoughtful type who carefully considers every word. But when he speaks, people listen.

Natural ability oozed from every one of Moseby's pores. His lithe, sculpted body was made for centre field. His combination of speed and power was a rarity, and his talent was recognized at an early age. When the time came, only one player — Atlanta's Bob Horner — was chosen ahead of him in the draft.

Ironically, when he was growing up, Moseby looked down his nose at baseball. Basketball was his game. High-school basketball games drew crowds, while baseball drew flies. "When you played basketball," he once said, "they talked about you, and they talked about you hard." Baseball was a way of making the days pass until evening brought a basketball game. "It was better than hangin' around home takin' out the garbage or shellin' peas."

After the baseball draft, though, the choice was clear. By signing with the Blue Jays, he was able to give back something to his parents, neither of whom was able to work by that time because of health reasons.

A year in rookie ball at Medicine Hat, another season of A ball in Dunedin, part of a year in Syracuse, and Moseby was in the big time. He was a child in an adult's body then, just as he is now — a babbling brook running through the clubhouse. At that stage in their development the Jays could easily afford to let a youngster like Moseby learn on the job. The team was going to lose anyway, so why not lose creatively?

Upshaw, one of fifteen brothers and sisters in the town of Blanco, Texas, on the other hand, was a product of hard work. He had been drafted in the fifth round in 1975 by the Yankees. Gillick, then a Yankee scout, signed him and still ranks Upshaw's development as one of his most satisfying scouting projects.

"Upshaw, when we signed him, was one of the crudest players I'd ever been involved with," recalled Gillick. "A diamond in the rough but a diamond that needed a lot of polishing. I went to Blanco — the school there was only about 180 kids — and watched him work out in the spring of 1975. He was also a football fullback, but he had some things baseball-wise that we liked. What we didn't know was what a determined worker he was. He was a guy who listened to instruction. But to get where he is today is just astounding from where he was then."

That's not to say that Moseby didn't have to work hard. When he began his minor-league apprenticeship, he did not have a strong throwing arm. He put an extra effort into becoming respectable in that area.

In 1983 Upshaw and Moseby took the American League by storm. Moseby hit .315 with eighteen homers and eighty-one RBIs. More significantly, he scored 104 runs, the first Blue Jay to score more than one hundred runs in a season. Upshaw hit .306 with twenty-seven homers and a club-record 104 RBIs, the first Jay to record one hundred RBIs in a season.

Moseby and Upshaw played four more years together but never again was it like it was in '83. Somewhere in the middle of 1984 Upshaw's power numbers started to fall, the result of a combination of factors. A bad wrist, torn stomach muscles and more attention from opposition pitchers contrived to keep Upshaw from again approaching his solid '83 season.

Moseby continued to shine offensively each year, but only in 1987 could it be said he matched his '83 output. In '87 Moseby hit .282 with twenty-six homers and ninety-six RBIs to go with 106 runs scored.

By the start of the 1988 season Fred McGriff was the new Toronto first baseman, and it was time for Upshaw to move on. He was traded to Cleveland near the end of spring training. "It was the hardest thing I ever had to do," said Moseby. "To say goodbye to a friend like that."

♦ WORLD SERIES DREAMS

But back in 1983 there were no such dark clouds on the horizon. There were no limits for Upshaw, Moseby or any of the other charmed Blue Jays. Despite their potential, the team played fitfully during April, finishing the month with just eight wins in eighteen games. But the team suddenly found itself in May, catapulting from sixth place at the month's beginning to the top of the heap.

May 29 was a truly historic day as the Jays moved into first place with a 6-1 win over Boston. Never in their previous six seasons had the Jays even dreamed of being near the lead this far into the season. For the next month the lead changed hands several times. Boston, Detroit, New York, Baltimore and, yes, Toronto all jockeyed for position. Then Toronto took over again on June 24 and held the lead for thirty-two consecutive days as pennant fever — albeit premature — gripped the city.

World Series dreams danced wildly through the minds of Blue Jays fans all over the country. Suddenly the upstart Blue Jays had replaced the Montreal Expos, the so-called "Team of the 80s," as the number-one baseball attraction in Canada.

One of the factors that had vaulted the Jays into the league's elite was a dramatically improved production from the designated hitter spot, a role shared by Toronto's answer to the Odd Couple.

Cliff Johnson, a nemesis of the Jays virtually since their inception, had been acquired from Oakland during the off-season in exchange for Al Woods. Jorge Orta arrived from Kansas City just before spring training. Johnson was a very gregarious type who loved to put on a show for the fans. Orta seldom uttered so much as a word and was thus dubbed "Silent Jorge." But between them they made plenty of noise with their bats, Johnson batting from the right side, Orta from the left. Toronto's designated hitters combined for thirty-four homers and 113 RBIs, most of them accounted for by Orta and Johnson. In 1982 Toronto's DHs had ranked fourteenth in a fourteen-team league. In 1983 they ranked number one.

♦ MURDER, SHE WROTE

By August 1, folks who didn't know a double from a double play were gobbling peanuts and CrackerJacks by the truckload and washing them down with some of Labatt's finest at Exhibition Stadium. Attendance soared with the hopes of the fans.

It was to this carnival atmosphere that Billy Martin brought his New York Yankees during the first week of August. The Yankees under the ownership of George Steinbrenner have long become accustomed to being at the centre of the bizarre and unusual but not even they were prepared for what happened on August 4, 1983.

Two days earlier a crowd of 45,102 — the largest ever to watch the Jays at home — had seen their heroes sweep the Yankees in a doubleheader. The Jays won the third game, and now it was Thursday and the series finale.

Not many folks who were there will ever recall the score (3-1 for New York), but they'll all remember the night that Dave Winfield killed a sea gull.

Winfield had been warming up in the outfield for the bottom of the fifth inning. Just before the first Blue Jays batter was set to step into the batter's box, Winfield wheeled and threw his practice ball towards the waiting ball boy. He scored a direct "gull's eye" on the head of an unsuspecting bird standing on the artificial surface. The gull never knew what hit it.

The ball boy came out with a towel, wrapped up the dead bird and took it away. But that was not to be the last of it. A Toronto police officer witnessed the incident and, suspecting foul play, decided to charge Winfield. Sea gulls are protected by law from willful killing by human beings.

"Intentional?" snorted Martin. "They wouldn't say that if they'd seen the way Winfield's been throwing. That's the first time he's hit the cutoff man all year."

Winfield was hauled away to a local police station to be booked. He eventually caught up with his teammates at the airport, having hitched a ride with Pat Gillick.

A day later red-faced police and city officials dropped the charges, and Metro Chairman Paul Godfrey even went so far as to apologize to Winfield personally a few days later at Yankee Stadium.

Said Martin: "Maybe we could have a memorial service for [the gull] before the game. Maybe we could bury him out there by the monuments, next to The Babe."

As Dave Winfield knows so well, flocks of sea gulls were as much a part of the scene at Exhibition Stadium as beer and hotdogs.

One Yankee fan had a novel idea: "How about an exchange? We could send youse Canadians a big old dead New York City rat."

There was a happy postscript to the ridiculous incident. As a peace offering, Winfield, through his involvement with a Minneapolis gallery, had a painting commissioned for donation to the Easter Seal foundation. It was auctioned off the following winter, realizing a profit of $32,000 for the charity.

♦ APOCALYPSE NOW

Baltimore, Detroit and New York stayed with the Blue Jays through July and August, but the turning point for the Jays occurred during a critical one-week stretch that became Toronto's version of *Apocalypse Now.*

Dave Collins was a spark plug in the Toronto offence, stealing thirty-one bases in 1983. In 1984 he set the team record for steals with sixty.

On August 15, the team left Toronto for an extraordinarily long and decisive road trip. Fourteen games in fourteen days in four cities — Cleveland, Boston, Baltimore and finally Detroit. Toronto won three of four contests in Cleveland and then split four games in Boston. When they arrived in Baltimore in the wee hours of August 23, they trailed the Orioles by two and a half games. Ahead lay the most important three games in the franchise history to date.

Toronto breezed through the opening game behind Luis Leal, winning 9-3 to cut the Orioles' lead to one and a half games. But it is the second game of this pivotal series that will live forever in the minds of die-hard Blue Jays fans. Bobby Cox swears he still has nightmares about it.

On that fateful evening Jim Clancy sailed into the ninth inning with a 3-1 lead. Toronto was on the verge of closing the gap to a scant half game. But the Orioles tied the game, scoring twice in the bottom half.

On to the tenth inning. In his desperate attempt to come back in the ninth, Oriole manager Joe Altobelli had run out of catchers. Lenn Sakata, a second baseman all his life, was nominated to wear the tools of ignorance and receive relief pitcher Tippy Martinez' offerings.

Cliff Johnson led off the Blue Jays' tenth with a solo home run to give Toronto a 4-3 lead. Barry Bonnell singled and, with the inexperienced Sakata behind the plate, eagerly awaited a chance to steal second. Stunningly, Martinez whirled and picked him off first base, Eddie Murray applying the tag. One out.

Fleet Dave Collins, who would steal thirty-one bases that season, kept the rally alive with a walk. Again, aware of Sakata's inexperience, Collins edged too far from first, and he, too, was picked off. Unbelievable. Two outs.

Willie Upshaw was next and he singled. Do you need to know more? Sad but true. Another Jay picked off and a rather unique place in baseball's record books for Martinez.

Years later Mike Flanagan, an Oriole pitcher then, still marvels at the feat. "I don't ever remember seeing Tippy pick anybody off. Three in one inning? Unbelievable."

Still, the Jays had a lead. Cox summoned Joey McLaughlin from the bull pen to protect it. As he took his warm-up throws, this press box announcement sent a shudder of anticipation down press row: "The Blue Jays are unbeaten in their last twelve consecutive extra-innings games," said the voice. "The last time Toronto lost was on a tenth-inning home run given up by Joey McLaughlin one year ago today. . . ."

Standing in the on-deck circle was Cal Ripken with mayhem on his mind. A moment later, he made a McLaughlin delivery disappear over the fence to tie the game. But the ultimate insult was left for Sakata to deliver. The reluctant catcher, a small man who would finish the season with just three home runs, delivered a three-run shot to win it for Baltimore.

The loss shattered the fragile confidence of a team so new to pennant pressure. Over the next seven nightmarish days the Jays lost three additional games in extra innings and two in the ninth to fall out of the race with a resounding thud.

♦ HELP WANTED

Their spirit largely broken, the Jays drifted through September, falling as far as eleven and a half games off the pace. They rallied to win five of their last seven to grab fourth place, nine games behind the champion Orioles.

As the players dispersed to their various winter homes that October, it was with bittersweet memories of the season. There was pride in the fact that for the first time the Jays had finished somewhere other than last place. Not only had they finished with a record better than .500 for the first time, they had also won eighty-nine games. But this was tempered by the knowledge that it could have been so much better.

Toronto had arrived as a power to be reckoned with in the American League East. The frightful collapse during the last week of August brought clearly into focus the club's most desperate need: a relief pitcher who could be counted on to protect a slim lead in the closing innings.

A sound diagnosis, to be sure, but one that proved far easier than the cure.

1984

THE TIGERS ROAR

It was time to investigate the free-agent market. Since 1975, when pitchers Andy Messersmith and Dave McNally successfully challenged baseball's reserve clause, each winter has produced a crop of players who have completed their previous contractual obligations. As a result, salaries have escalated astronomically as teams try for the "quick fix," believing that a Reggie Jackson or a Pete Rose or, yes, a Kirk Gibson could bring them a championship.

During the winter that preceded the 1984 season, the Blue Jays felt they were a player or two from a championship. Specifically, they needed a bull-pen closer, and one of the best in the game happened to be available. Rich "Goose" Gossage's style was as subtle as a belch. He was the Mister T of relief pitchers: "Here it is, sucker; hit it if you can," seemed to be his slogan. And not many hitters could catch up with his ninety-five-mile-per-hour fastball. With the New York Yankees he had been the prototypical short reliever. Seattle Mariner Tom Paciorek once described Gossage this way: "There's smoke coming out of his nose and his cap is down over his eyes and he's so big and hulking. You need a cape to face Gossage, not a baseball bat."

Jimmy Key was the big surprise of the 1984 training camp, earning a job on the Blue Jays' pitching staff after less than two full years in the minor leagues.

Gossage was a longshot. In the end, the Blue Jays offered him a three-year package that would have paid him $7.5 million, including bonuses and incentives. Even though the Toronto offer was attractive financially, on January 6, 1984, acknowledging the lure of southern California, Gossage signed a five-year deal with the San Diego Padres that paid him a guaranteed $6 million.

"They were very serious," Gossage said of the Blue Jays. "They made a hell of an effort. But there were a lot of things involved."

♦ SPINNING THEIR TIRES

There was another reliever available, and the Jays quickly went to Plan B. Performing on a Chicago White Sox bull-pen staff that saved games by committee,

Rich "Goose" Gossage was always an imposing sight for opposition hitters. The Blue Jays bid for his services but lost out to San Diego.

Dennis Lamp had saved fifteen games in 1983 for the West Division champs. On January 10, 1984, he signed on with Toronto as the team's first front-line free agent.

He was billed as a short-relief specialist, but he knew and the Jays' management knew that role was not entirely suited to his talents. He was not a classic strikeout pitcher but a sinker-baller who relied on his defence to convert ground balls into double plays. As the Jays would see, ground balls often become base hits. Base hits, in the bottom of the ninth with the winning run on base, just will not do.

Ironically, the Detroit Tigers had the same problem. They waited until near the end of spring training before making their move. They traded outfielder Glenn Wilson and third baseman John Wockenfuss to Philadelphia for journeyman Dave Bergman and a left-handed pitcher named Willie Hernandez with a career total of twenty-seven saves in seven seasons.

It was a sign of things to come. The Tigers, it seemed, were a team of destiny in '84. Everything they touched turned to gold. Hernandez blossomed in short relief, converting thirty-three save opportunities into thirty-two saves. He won nine games and compiled a microscopic 1.92 ERA on his way to being named the American League's most valuable player.

On the other hand, Toronto's makeshift bull-pen arrangement started to unravel as early as opening day in Seattle. Starter Jim Clancy nursed a 2-1 lead into the eighth inning and left with four outs to go. Lamp couldn't hold the lead, and the Jays lost 3-2 in ten innings.

Still, the Jays wasted little time in establishing they were ready to contend, with a 13-9 record at the end of April and a 32-15 record at the end of May. The problem was, the Tigers were off in a league by themselves with a phenomenal record of thirty-five wins in their first forty games.

Toronto had taken over second place on April 28, and that's where they stayed for the rest of the way, spending 156 days looking up at Detroit and cursing their bad luck. They played the best baseball in the history of the franchise and ended the season with nothing to show for it.

During the winter preceding the '84 season, outfielder Barry Bonnell had been dealt to Seattle for left-handed pitcher Bryan Clark. Clark was to fill a much-needed role in the bull pen. The Jays hadn't had a quality left-handed reliever in two years, and Clark had a reputation for being death on left-handed hitters. Two developments scuttled this plan.

First, Clark was terrible. Whatever talent he'd had before had deserted him. He could not find the plate with any of his pitches. Patiently manager Bobby Cox waited through spring training for Clark to start to show his true stuff.

Second, a youngster named Jimmy Key, who had been ticketed for AAA Syracuse in the preseason planning, was making life miserable for opposition hitters and had the Blue Jays management scratching its collective head.

♦ EARNING HIS DREAM

Years before, Carol Key, a secretary for NASA in Huntsville, Alabama, had smiled indulgently when her ten-year-old son, sprawled in front of the TV set watching baseball, had informed her quite seriously that someday she'd be watching him pitch on TV. But perhaps Jimmy's mother had underestimated his resolve. Throughout high school Jimmy maintained interest in basketball and baseball, and when he was seventeen, the Chicago White Sox drafted him. But Jimmy Key already had his route to the big leagues mapped out.

"I told the White Sox scout that I had no intention of signing before college," said Key. "A kid that age is too immature to head off on his own. I had the chance for a full scholarship at Clemson, where they had a great baseball program with a guaranteed education."

In his senior year at Clemson, his 9-3 record with a 2.79 ERA caught the attention of the Blue Jays, who drafted him in the third round. "I was told by scouts in the organization it was up to me. . . . That if I pitched well, I'd get my chance to make the big team relatively fast."

Key started five games at Medicine Hat in 1982 but was quickly elevated to Florence, South Carolina, of the South Atlantic League. He split his second professional season between Knoxville and Syracuse and was impressive enough to get an invitation to spring training in '84.

BLUE JA

He arrived in Dunedin that spring prepared to wring as much experience as he could from his first big-league camp before being sent off, inevitably, to Syracuse for more seasoning. "The fact that I had come to camp not really counting on making the team probably worked to my benefit," he reflected later. "I didn't feel any pressure at all until later on when I realized they were giving me serious consideration. By that time it was too late to be nervous."

It was coming down to the crunch when the Jays headed off for the West Coast and a series of exhibition games in Vancouver. Before they left Vancouver for one last tune-up in Portland, Oregon, against the Mariners, Key and Stan Clarke were sent back to Dunedin to join the Syracuse Chiefs. The next day in Portland, Bryan Clark pitched poorly. After the game Cox, Pat Gillick and some of the scouts huddled again and came to a new determination: send out Clark, recall Key.

"It was a nightmare," said Key. "It had been a terrible flight back [to Dunedin]. The next morning I reported to the minor-league complex, and Gord Ash called me into the office. I figured it was going to be a pep talk, since I'd been sent out on the last day and all. At first I thought he was pulling my leg when he told me they wanted me in Seattle. The whole flight back there were a million things running through my head."

Key had never pitched out of the bull pen — he'd always been a starting pitcher — but he appeared in sixty-three games as a relief pitcher that first season, compiling a 4-5 record with a 4.65 ERA and ten saves. Later he looked back on it as an ideal way to break into the big time. "I experienced the highest highs and the lowest lows in the bull pen. It taught me how to handle difficult situations. In the bull pen, one night you'd walk into a critical situation and pitch out of it to save a game and you'd feel great. The next night you go out with a two-run lead, throw one pitch and the guy hits a game-winning homer. You grow up quickly in that situation."

By the next spring Key was in the starting rotation, and by the time the all-star break rolled around, he had impressed Sparky Anderson enough that the Detroit skipper named him to the all-star team. He finished with a 14-6 record and a 3.00 ERA, fourth best in the league.

In 1987 Key finished second in the Cy Young award voting, just behind Boston's Roger Clemens.

♦ A PRECIOUS TALENT

Tony Fernandez arrived in the big leagues to stay in 1984, forcing the Jays to trade Alfredo Griffin after the season.

But in 1984 Key was just another wide-eyed rookie trying to hang on. Nor was he the only rookie to make a big impression. This was the long-awaited debut season for Tony Fernandez. His arrival had been delayed somewhat by a slow-to-heal wrist injury sustained the previous year, but shortly after his first game on May 22 it became apparent he was in Toronto to stay.

Fernandez had a rare and precious talent. By the end of that first year he was already being compared to Ozzie Smith, the acrobatic shortstop for the St. Louis Cardinals and the man by whose standards all other shortstops are judged.

Beyond his exquisite fielding talent, Fernandez was a mirror image of Rod Carew at the plate.

As a youngster growing up in San Pedro de Macoris he was obsessed with baseball, haunting Tetelo Varga Stadium near his home from dawn till dusk. Shirtless, barefoot and with a glove moulded from old cardboard, the kid with the head too large for his body would field ground ball after ground ball — as many as 400 in a day. He became such a nuisance the stadium staff gave him a job cleaning the place.

"He said he would be leaving for school in the morning," recalled his mother, Andrea. "But he never took his clean clothes. He would come home and tell me he forgot to put them on, but I always knew he had gone to the ball park."

As the 1983 season came to a close, a trade of either Griffin or Garcia would be necessary to keep everyone happy. The next winter Griffin went to Oakland in the deal that brought Bill Caudill to Toronto.

♦ CLOSE ENCOUNTER

While the Jays were consigned to second place most of the season, the year was not without its dramatic moments. We take you now to Tiger Stadium. The date was June 4, 1984, and for the first time that season the Jays and the Tigers got a chance to square off, the teams with the two best records in baseball.

The Tigers held a healthy four and a half game lead, but with four games head-to-head it was an opportunity for the Jays to make a new season of it. As it turned out, it was the closest to a pennant race the East would see that season.

Toronto's two prized rookies: Tony Fernandez (far left) *and Jimmy Key* (near left).

Right: *When the Jays couldn't land "Goose" Gossage, they settled for Dennis Lamp to anchor their bull pen.*

The opening game, on national TV in the United States, was a classic. Blue Jays fans had gotten a taste of pennant fever the previous year and wanted more. For one night, at least, they got it.

Toronto jumped away to a 3-0 lead on a solo homer by Upshaw in the second inning and a two-run shot by Bell in the sixth. In the Detroit seventh Stieb hit Chet Lemon with a pitch, Bergman followed with a single and then Howard Johnson ripped a three-run homer to tie the game.

On to the tenth inning. Reliever Jimmy Key, after getting out of a Dennis Lamp-made jam in the ninth, created one of his own in the tenth. Cox again signalled to the bull pen. There were two out and two on when Bergman stepped in to face Roy Lee Jackson.

Jackson got two quick strikes and then the chess game began. Bergman fouled off four pitches in succession. Then Jackson missed on three straight deliveries to bring the count full. Bergman fouled off three more pitches. The at-bat was in its ninth minute. At one point Bergman turned to Buck Martinez and asked if there was a curfew in effect. Jackson delivered again. Bergman swung. The ball was in the air. Jesse Barfield drifted back towards the right-field seats, but he had no chance. The Tigers won 6-3.

The Jays came back to win two of the next three in Detroit, but never would they get any closer than they were that Monday night. By the time September rolled around, Detroit was home and cooled out. They eventually won the division by fifteen games.

There were plenty of performances to savor: Doyle Alexander's seventeen-win season, a year after being declared washed up by George Steinbrenner. George Bell's twenty-six homers. Dave Collins' .308 batting average and sixty stolen bases. Lloyd Moseby's team-leading ninety-two RBIs. Dave Stieb's 2.83 ERA.

But the team was hungry for a championship, and no individual accomplishment would replace the empty feeling that comes with second place.

BLUE JAYS

1985

THAT CHAMPIONSHIP SEASON

"It is designed to break your heart. The game begins in the spring, when everything else begins again and it blossoms in the summer, filling the afternoons and evenings, and then as the chill rains come, it stops and leaves you to face the fall alone."

— A. BARTLETT GIAMATTI

On a frozen January afternoon in 1985 Sparky Anderson was delivering a lecture in Psychology 101 over the telephone from his home in Thousand Oaks, California. "It's like this," the manager of the defending World Series champion Detroit Tigers was saying. "You've got a ball club and you're playin' pretty good ball. You're goin' along and you come to the eighth inning with a two-run lead and you lose. Okay, those things happen. Then it happens three times in one week. Six or seven times in a month. All of a sudden your guys are sayin', 'How many runs do we have to score to win?' It starts to beat them down.

"Then you go out and get a guy like Bill Caudill or a guy like Gary Lavelle and you start winning those 3-2 and 5-4 games. You get to the ninth inning with a one-run lead, and everybody knows you're gonna win. It changes the whole team's outlook. All of a sudden a .300 hitter doesn't mind bunting a runner over because he realizes one run might be all it takes."

♦ A POSITIVE FEELING

Bill Caudill never lived up to expectations but his arrival brought a fresh confidence to the team.

For two years the Blue Jays had possessed all but one of the elements they needed to put together a championship season. They had speed. They had defence. They had power. They had pitching. What they did not have was a no-nonsense bull-pen closer, and that lack had had a demoralizing effect on the young Jays.

And now, as the 1985 season approached, that hole had been plugged.

On December 8, 1984, at the conclusion of the winter meetings in Dallas, the

Jays announced a deal that brought Bill Caudill to Toronto from the Oakland Athletics in exchange for Alfredo Griffin and Dave Collins. A few weeks later Pat Gillick closed another deal with the San Francisco Giants, sending Jim Gott and minor-leaguer Augie Schmidt west, swapped for lefty reliever Gary Lavelle.

In the previous three seasons, one in Oakland and two in Seattle, the swashbuckling Caudill, just twenty-eight, had saved eighty-eight games for noncontending teams. Lavelle, thirty-six, with 127 career saves, was the all-time Giants' leader in that category.

Long before he had signed a whopping five-year contract with Toronto that could pay him as much as $8 million and long before he had thrown his first pitch as a Blue Jay, Caudill had started doing the job for which he'd been hired. In town for a charity function, Caudill was greeted enthusiastically by a crowd of 2,000 and immediately promised a World Series for Toronto the next fall. This was music to the beleaguered city's ears.

By the time training camp opened, the Caudill-Lavelle tandem had everyone on the team thinking in terms of a championship. From the very first day there was the sense that this was a team with a purpose, with the emphasis on the word "team."

♦ PSYCHOLOGICAL GAMES

Years before, one of Peter Bavasi's favorite themes was "selling the sizzle." In a sense, that's what Bill Caudill and Gary Lavelle contributed in the spring of '85. They sold the sizzle. They sold it to the fans and they sold it to their teammates.

In the hard glare of history neither man came close to fulfilling the promise. Unknown even to himself, about the time he was traded to Toronto Caudill had been struck by a rare form of viral arthritis that left him in a weakened condition, unable to throw his fastball past even the most feeble of hitters. And Lavelle's pitching elbow was all but shot, finally giving out on him late in the season. Caudill had fourteen saves, none of them in the last two months of the season. Lavelle finished with eight saves. But there is no denying the psychological lift these men gave to the Blue Jays.

Years later Bobby Cox still believes the two men were the keys to the championship season, even if they did not contribute materially down the stretch. "When you don't have a bull pen, it infects the entire team," said Cox in 1988. "It infects the starters, who try too hard. It infects the regular players, who start to believe that somehow they'll find a way to lose. And it infects the manager, who starts managing out of fear. Caudill and Lavelle created a positive feeling that carried on through the season. They didn't do well, as it turned out, but the mind frame they established remained in place until Tom Henke came up from the minors in late July and became the closer we so desperately needed."

While spring training victories don't necessarily mean much, the Blue Jays' success in the spring of '85 was indicative of the prevailing mood. The Jays won their first nine exhibition games in Florida, eventually finishing the Grapefruit League schedule with nineteen wins and nine losses.

Gary Lavelle came to Toronto as the San Francisco Giants all-time saves leader.

When the regular schedule started, the Blue Jays won just three of their first seven to fall three and a half games off the pace set by the Tigers, who won their first seven in a row. This conjured up memories of the year previous, when Detroit roared away from everybody in April, never to be caught.

Not this time, however. The Jays rattled off four wins in a row, lost three, then won seven more in succession to stay within striking range of the Tigers. On April 30 they moved into first place for the first time, fell back, then took over first place for good on May 13.

♦ IN FIRST TO STAY

There were some tight squeezes over the next five months, but never did the Jays fall out of first place from that day forward.

Of course, the bull-pen situation was just one aspect of Toronto's "Drive of '85." But it was a major contributor. When the season was finished, the Jays' bull pen was rated the best in baseball, having saved forty-seven games while winning thirty-five.

Alexander turned out to be the stopper on the starting staff, winning seventeen games for the second straight year. Stieb, while leading the league with a stingy 2.48 ERA, won just fourteen. So did Key. The major surprise, and the man who eventually was named the club's pitcher of the year, was Lamp, who rolled up an 11-0 record working middle relief.

While they didn't always agree with him, the Blue Jays universally respected manager Bobby Cox.

Leal was replaced in the rotation by Tom Filer, who had signed with the Toronto organization as a minor-league free agent the previous winter. All Filer did was rack up a 7-0 record until a tender elbow sidelined him in September.

For Clancy it was a disappointing season. He did not return from his appendectomy until the end of April and then suffered through another stint on the disabled list with tendinitis in his shoulder from the end of July into September.

The hallmark of the Toronto offence in '85 was the consistency it received from all sections of the lineup. Nine players had fifty or more RBIs during the season, and five players were in double figures in game-winning RBIs. At the forefront of the assault were the Killer Bees, Bell and Barfield. Bell knocked in ninety-five runs with twenty-seven homers while Barfield drove in eighty-four with twenty-eight homers. Fernandez, in his first full season as the Jays' shortstop, was perhaps the most valuable player on the team. In addition to his superb defence, he hit .289 with fifty-one RBIs despite batting ninth in the order.

At the end of May the Blue Jays' lead stood at four games. By June 7 they had stretched it to six and a half before they went into a skid. They lost nine of their next eleven, including six in a row, reducing the lead to two and a half games on the 18th. But that was as close as the Yankees would get until September.

♦ THE GREATEST PLAY

Just before the all-star break, the Jays went west for an eleven-day trip. After splitting four games in Oakland, they headed for Seattle. On July 8, Dave Stieb defeated Mike Moore 4-0 at the KingDome, and then the next night Filer made his debut with the Jays, replacing Leal in the rotation.

Just before the game Gillick announced that designated hitter Len Matuszek had been traded to the Los Angeles Dodgers for Al Oliver, a career .300 hitter who would take over the designated hitter duties from the left side.

But the big news of the evening occurred in the third inning. That's when Buck Martinez made the play of his career, a play that is still talked about. "Greatest play I've ever seen," said Blue Jays vice-president Bobby Mattick, who has been in professional baseball for more than fifty years.

Seattle slugger Gorman Thomas was at the plate with one out in the third inning of a scoreless ball game. Phil Bradley was on second base, the result of a single and a balk called against Filer. Thomas singled sharply to right field. Despite the fact that Jesse Barfield — possessor of one of the strongest, most accurate arms in all of baseball — was charging the ball, Bradley was sent home by Seattle third-base coach Jim Mahoney.

It was no contest. Martinez grabbed Barfield's throw and turned to face Bradley, formerly a quarterback at the University of Missouri. Bradley did the only thing he could: he put his shoulder down and went into his football mode, slamming into Martinez like a runaway freight train.

"While I was waiting for Bradley to hit me," said Martinez the next day, "I had this flashback to my first big-league game [when] I was hit the same way by Bob Allison. Knocked me out cold."

This time he remained conscious, but just barely. The force of the Bradley hit tore all the ligaments in Martinez' right ankle and fractured his right leg. But Bradley was out.

Now on his back and dazed, Martinez saw Thomas breaking for third base. Martinez tried to throw him out, but the ball flew out of his hand at an odd angle, ending up in short left field, where George Bell picked it up. By this time Thomas was on his way home, expecting to score a "gimmee" run with Martinez prone at the plate.

Bell threw the ball anyway. It bounced once, virtually hitting Martinez in the glove. He squeezed it, half turned and banged Thomas on the leg a split-second before he touched the plate. The play went into the books as a 9-2-7-2 double play, the oddest combination of numbers you'll ever see in a score book.

"Guts and instinct," said manager Bobby Cox. "That's what that play was. I've never seen anything to compare with it."

Martinez' season was finished. He did come back in 1986 for one last season before he retired, but it was all anti-climactic after that night in Seattle.

♦ THE ANTHEM BLUES

Very few teams ever get to a division championship without being severely tested at some point, and the Jays were no exception in '85. On September 12 they arrived in New York for a critical four-game series, leading the Yankees by two and a half games.

Aside from promoting Henke, the only late-season change the Jays made in preparation for the stretch run was to reacquire Cliff Johnson from Texas in exchange for pitcher Matt Williams.

On the first night Toronto's worst fears were realized. Leading 4-1 in the seventh inning, Tony Fernandez and Damaso Garcia botched a double play that would have ended a three-up, three-down inning. Instead, it turned into a six-run uprising that led to a 7-5 New York win, cutting the lead to one and a half games.

Almost as insulting as the loss was the fact that the Yankee Stadium fans had loudly booed the Canadian anthem, angering even the Americans on the team. "It was the most bush-league thing I've ever heard in baseball," said Johnson, a Texan. "They can yell whatever they want at the players, but when they insult a whole country, that's unspeakable."

Even George Steinbrenner was embarrassed. The following evening, he had the stadium announcer read a flowery tribute to Canadian-American relations that has since become a fixture in Yankee Stadium before each game between the Jays and the Yankees.

The Jays responded to good old Bronx hospitality by winning the second game of the series 3-2 to regain their two-and-a-half game bulge.

On Saturday night, the anthem blues continued but in another vein. The Yankees handed the microphone to lounge singer Mary O'Dowd, who wailed her way into infamy, forgetting first the words, then the entire melody of "O Canada." It may have been the most excruciating rendition of any anthem ever offered for public consumption.

The Jays eventually had the Yankees singing a sad refrain of their own when they beat the New Yorkers 7-4 behind Jimmy Key's complete game, Jesse Barfield's homer and two-RBI performances from Johnson and Moseby.

In the final game the Blue Jays put a hammer lock on the Big Apple and squeezed out every ounce of juice, winning 8-5. Toronto broke it open with six unanswered runs in the third inning. That gave the Jays a four-and-a-half game lead, and Steinbrenner was livid. "We have been out-played, we have been out-managed, we have been out-front-officed and we have been out-ownered," said the Yankee owner. No one was prepared to argue with him.

The race was not over. The Yankees still had one last shot at the Jays in Toronto on the final weekend of the season. It was a three-game series, and the Yankees needed to win all three to tie. Toronto needed to win just one.

The largest Blue Jays crowd ever — 47,686 — showed up on Friday, October 4, hoping to be a part of history. What they witnessed was certainly high drama. But not the history they were expecting.

It was cold, and by the late innings, it was raining. Raining hard. But as the ninth inning dawned, the Jays clung to a 3-2 lead. Tom Henke got the first two outs. The crowd was in full voice, oblivious to the weather. Two strikes on Yankees' catcher Butch Wynegar, the championship one pitch away. The roar was deafening.

Then . . . silence.

The ball rocketed off Wynegar's bat into the deep, dark night beyond the right-field fence. Tie game. "When I was rounding the bases, you could have heard a pin drop," said Wynegar later. "It was an eerie feeling." While the Jays and their fans were still trying to digest this development, Rickey Henderson

In addition to his superb hitting, Cliff Johnson was one of the Blue Jays fans' favorites.

walked, bringing Don Mattingly to the plate. Mattingly lofted a lazy fly ball to centre field. Moseby waited under it. He tapped his glove in anticipation of the third out. Then he dropped the ball. The Yankees won 4-3.

♦ DOYLE'S MASTERPIECE

The scene shifts to Saturday, October 5. The focus was on right-handed pitcher Doyle Alexander, who faced a phalanx of left-handed Yankee power. The weather didn't favor the Jays; a stiff wind was blowing out to the inviting right-field fence. But it was Toronto's left-handed power that lit up the gloomy afternoon. Ernie Whitt set the tone with a towering home run in the bottom of the second inning. Moseby and Upshaw followed with back-to-back homers with one out in the third.

"From there it was just a matter of giving the ball to Doyle and letting him do his thing," said manager Cox. Pitching with uncanny control, Alexander limited the Yankees to five hits, and remarkably, not one ball was hit into right field, where the wind and the fences beckoned.

Then, with two outs in the ninth, Ron Hassey swung at an Alexander offering. The ball looped on a high arc into left field, and the fans in the swollen stadium held their breath. The ball flew softly, harmlessly out over Tony Fernandez' head in a losing battle against the wind. Left-fielder George Bell came in a few steps and waited while 44,608 hearts pounded.

As the ball nestled into Bell's glove — he later said he squeezed it so hard he could feel the laces through the leather — he fell to his knees in exultation. At precisely 4:28 p.m. on October 5, 1985, the roar was deafening.

Eight years, five months, twenty-eight days and three hours after Bill Singer had flung that first pitch past Ralph Garr, the Blue Jays were the best team in the American League East.

On the same day in Kansas City, the Royals beat the Oakland Athletics to clinch the American League West. It would be Toronto and Kansas City in the playoffs, seven games head to head for the American League pennant.

UPSHAW
26

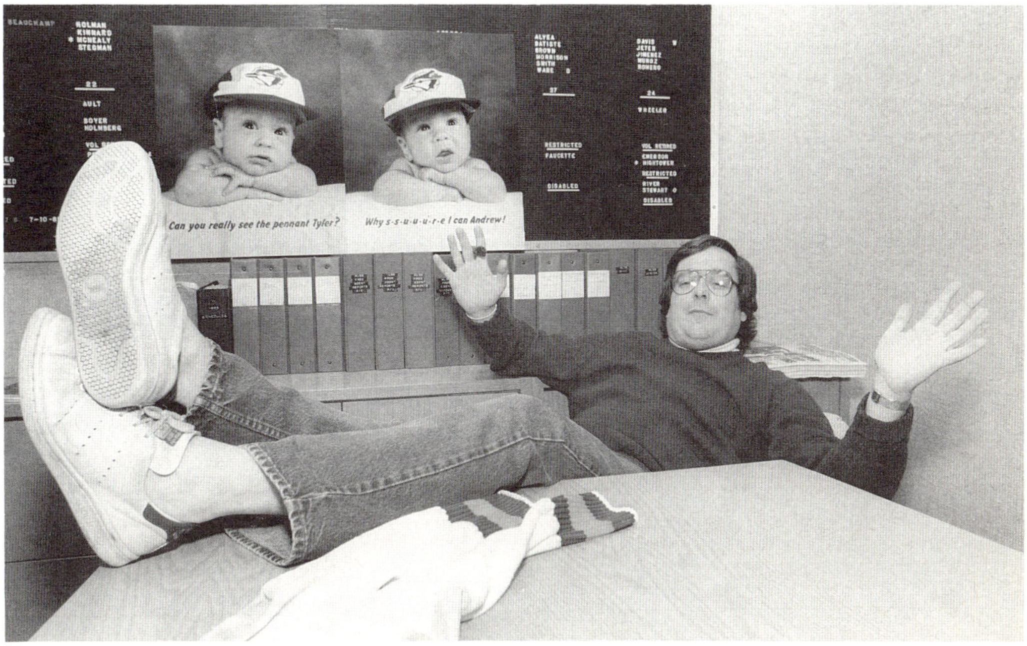

Left: *Willie Upshaw and Damaso Garcia rush to the mound to hug Doyle Alexander after the final out in the 1985 division-clinching victory over New York.*

Top: *Seconds after he clutched the final out, George Bell celebrated with Tony Fernandez in left field.*

Bottom: *Club vice-president Paul Beeston vowed not to wear socks until the Blue Jays won the World Series.*

Al Oliver is mobbed at home plate after driving home Lloyd Moseby from second base to give Toronto a 6-5 victory and a 2-0 series lead over Kansas City.

♦ THE PLAYOFFS

Game 1 at Toronto, October 8. Toronto 6, Kansas City 1.

Appropriately enough, the story of the club's first foray into postseason play was all Dave Stieb's. Stieb was the team's first marquee player as far back as the dark days of 1979, but he was seldom better than in this opening game against Charlie Leibrandt and the Royals.

Not even a stripper named Juanita who flounced out of the stands and drooled on his neck as he warmed up in the second inning could distract Stieb from his appointment this day.

Stieb limited Kansas City to just three hits through eight innings, and not once did he allow a base runner to advance past second base. Meanwhile, his teammates, led by two-RBI performances from Tony Fernandez and Ernie Whitt, staked Stieb to a five-run lead after three innings and made it 6-0 in the fourth. Kansas City broke the shutout in the ninth against Tom Henke.

Game 2 at Toronto, October 9. Toronto 6, Kansas City 5.

The tumultuous day was over. On a stereo down the hall Tina Turner was wailing, "We don't need another hero . . ." and in walked Al Oliver, his timing impeccable as always. On this day the Blue Jays had needed every hero they could lay their hands on. But they all had to stand in line behind the thirty-nine-year-old Oliver, who had driven home Lloyd Moseby from second base with a two-out, tenth-inning single to give Toronto a 6-5 victory.

There were a dozen plot lines in this nerve snapper, but none so dramatic as

Oliver's. With the game on the line he stepped into the box against Royals' reliever Dan Quisenberry and flailed futilely at the first pitch. "I think Quisenberry smelled a little blood," said Oliver.

On the next pitch Oliver made himself look absolutely foolish with a mighty swing and a miss, nearly falling down in the process. "I tried to do a Reggie Jackson number, but that terrible swing snapped me back to reality. I'm not Reggie Jackson. A single would win the ball game.

"The next pitch was a ball. Close, but outside, and I watched it. I was starting to get back in sync. Then I fouled one off to right field, and I was comfortable. The next pitch I just reached out and popped it into left field."

So much had happened to lead Oliver to his moment.

Kansas City had jumped out quickly in the third against starter Jimmy Key on a rare Willie Wilson two-run homer. Jim Sundberg made it 3-0 with an RBI double in the fourth inning. Toronto got a run back in the fourth on Cliff Johnson's double that scored George Bell. In the sixth inning Jesse Barfield's thirty-two-hop single up the middle with two outs scored both Johnson and Bell to tie the game.

Toronto took a 4-3 lead in the eighth inning when Moseby singled, stole second, went to third on Sundberg's throwing error and scored on Bell's sacrifice fly. In the ninth, however, Pat Sheridan stroked a game-tying homer against Tom Henke to send it into extra innings.

In the Kansas City tenth Wilson singled to lead off. Two outs later he stole second base, then scored on Frank White's controversial sinking line drive single that Moseby figured he had caught. No matter. In the tenth, Fernandez led off with a single, moved to second on Garcia's ground out, then scored on Moseby's single to right, running through third base coach Jimy Williams' stop sign in the process. Moseby moved to second when Steve Balboni missed a pick-off attempt at first base, and that put Oliver squarely in the spotlight to deliver his game-winner. Lights out, Royals.

Game 3 at Kansas City, October 11. Kansas City 6, Toronto 5.

Before the series started, Bobby Cox had said, "There's no way we're going to let George Brett beat us," but somewhere in the backs of their minds the Blue Jays had conceded a game to Brett, the superb Kansas City third baseman and a clutch performer throughout his career.

This was George's night, pure and simple. He hit two home runs, scored three times, drove in four and made a brilliant defensive play as the Royals won 6-5. Typically, he got his biggest charge out of the defensive play that cut down a run at the plate after snatching a hot smash from the bat of Lloyd Moseby.

Meanwhile, the Jays erupted for a five-run fifth inning against Bret Saberhagen to assume a 5-2 lead, which they couldn't hold. Jim Sundberg homered in the fifth, and then Brett's second homer tied it at 5-5 in the sixth. Steve Balboni delivered the game-winning hit, a single in the eighth against Jim Clancy, who was making a rare and reluctant relief appearance.

Left: *Dave Stieb watched in disbelief as Jim Sundberg's harmless-looking fly ball bounced off the top of the right field fence for a game-winning, three-run triple in Game 7.*

Right: *Damaso Garcia reflected the mood in the Blue Jay club-house after losing Game 5 in Kansas City.*

Game 4 at Kansas City, October 12. Toronto 3, Kansas City 1.

Attempting to atone for his early exit in Game 1, Leibrandt worked eight shutout innings before the roof fell in in the ninth. The Royals had scored in the sixth inning after a daring move by Toronto manager Bobby Cox had backfired. Cox ordered an intentional walk to Brett with runners at first and third to fill the bases with nobody out. The unconventional strategy came into question, at least in part, when Stieb walked Hal McRae to score a run.

That's the way the score remained until the ninth, when Toronto scored three times. Leibrandt committed the cardinal sin of walking free-swinger Damaso Garcia to lead off the inning, then gave up the game-tying hit, a double by Moseby. Al Oliver then delivered the winning runs with a two-run double against Quisenberry to assume a commanding 3-1 lead in the series.

Game 5 at Kansas City, October 13. Kansas City 2, Toronto 0.

The fifth game can be summed up in two words: Danny Jackson. The talented Kansas City left-hander stifled the Blue Jays with an eight-hit shutout, stranding eight men on base in the process. The Royals scored runs in the first and second innings against Jimmy Key and that was more than enough to send the series back to Toronto for at least one more game.

Game 6 at Toronto, October 15. Kansas City 5, Toronto 3.

Once again the theme was familiar. The Blue Jays had plenty of base runners but couldn't deliver them across the plate in sufficient numbers. A trio of Royals pitchers — Mark Gubicza, Bud Black and Quisenberry — stranded nine Toronto base runners. The first inning was typical: Toronto put runners at second and third with none out, but scored only one run and that on a double-play ball hit by Rance Mulliniks.

For the second time in the series Kansas City got to Alexander for five runs, and that was more than they needed. Brett hit another homer, giving him three in the series against Alexander, McRae drove in two runs and Buddy Biancalana got into the act with an RBI double.

Game 7 at Toronto, October 16. Kansas City 6, Toronto 2.

In his autobiography *Tomorrow I'll Be Perfect*, Dave Stieb recalls "looking over my shoulder and watching a harmless fly ball refuse to drop out of the October night sky" and "the dagger deep in my gut when the ball popped off the bar on the top of the fence." And for millions across Canada it caused heartache of the most painful sort.

It was the sixth inning of this decisive game. The Royals led Stieb and the Jays 2-1. Already Jim Sundberg, a thirteen-year veteran performing in his first playoff and a man universally admired for his defensive skills, not his bat, had done damage to Stieb, delivering Kansas City's first run with a single in the second inning. Pat Sheridan's solo homer in the fourth had made it 2-0. Willie Upshaw had doubled home Damaso Garcia with Toronto's run in the fifth.

Now, Sundberg was back at the plate in the sixth. George Brett had walked with one out. Then Stieb hit Hal McRae, got another out on a spectacular fielding play by Tony Fernandez, then walked Steve Balboni. Two men out, bases loaded.

Sundberg took a pitch, a ball outside. Stieb delivered a second time, and Sundberg lifted it up into the breeze blowing out toward right field, plunging that dagger into Dave Stieb's gut. Right fielder Jesse Barfield leaped up the wall but the ball bounced above his glove, dropping back to earth for a triple. It was 5-1 on the way to a final 6-2.

Bret Saberhagen, eventually the Cy Young award winner and the World Series MVP for 1985, shut down the Jays the rest of the way. It turned into a miracle season of sorts for the Royals. In the World Series against St. Louis, they fell behind 3-1 again, only to stage a courageous comeback to take the series in seven games.

For Toronto, however, the season was over. The dream was dead, and the game "designed to break your heart" had done its job magnificently. The dread chill rains had come. We faced the fall alone.

1986

HEADING FOR A FALL

It has been said that it's much easier to win a championship than to defend one. That is particularly true of baseball in the 1980s. The Kansas City Royals were the only team to win full-season division championships in back-to-back seasons in this decade. They did it in 1984-85. The Yankees won the American League East in both 1980 and 1981, but the '81 victory was partly a result of the split-season concept adopted because of the strike. No team had won consecutive World Series titles since the Yankees did it in 1977-78.

It didn't take long for the postchampionship blues to set in with the Blue Jays. The first setback occurred just five days after the '85 team was eliminated by the Kansas City Royals. That's when Bobby Cox announced he was heading home to Atlanta to be the Braves' general manager.

Ted Turner had offered Cox a five-year contract "for more money than I could have imagined. And it was a chance to be with my family on a full-time basis. I hated to leave Toronto, but the offer was too good to be true."

A few days later Pat Gillick announced his new manager — to no one's surprise, third-base coach Jimy Williams was taking over. Williams had been with the Jays since 1979, and he knew the entire organization from top to bottom. Before he came to Toronto he had been a successful minor-league manager in the California Angels' chain.

Jimy Williams, third-base coach for six seasons, was named manager after Bobby Cox left to become general manager of the Atlanta Braves.

Williams was the fourth manager in the team's history, and it can be argued that he had the toughest assignment of the four. Roy Hartsfield and Bobby Mattick both knew their teams would not be winners. So did the front office and the fans. Theirs was more a developmental role. Cox, in 1982, took over a young, talented, enthusiastic team, a hungry team, and took them to the top.

The team that Williams took over was more mature, more secure financially. Most of its top stars were now being rewarded rather handsomely. They were coming off a ninety-nine-win season. How would they take to a new manager?

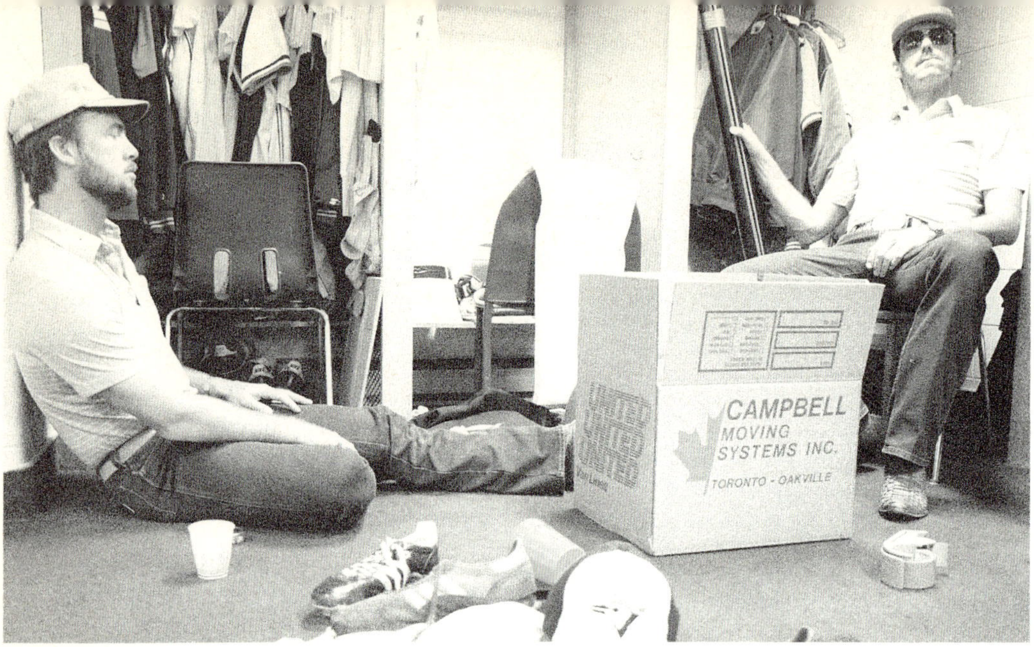

When Bobby Cox came back to Toronto in July, 1986, for an old-timers game, he took pitchers Jim Acker and Doyle Alexander back to Atlanta with him in separate trades.

"There are a couple of ways to look at it," said Williams before training camp. "Is it easier to go to a club which is not supposed to win and manage it, or is it easier to remain with a club that won ninety-nine games and is expected to win again? I don't know the answer to that. I think realistically if you had asked me that a few months ago, I probably would have stated that it would be easier to go to a club that wasn't expected to win — except in the case of the Toronto Blue Jays. I guess that's why I made the decision I did.

"We didn't have any player hit thirty home runs last year or score one hundred runs or drive in one hundred runs. We didn't have a pitcher win twenty games or save twenty games. That suggests to me there are still some big seasons ahead for some of these guys."

He was right. There were plenty of big seasons ahead. Bell. Barfield. Fernandez. Unfortunately, there were too many less-than-big seasons on the horizon, as well.

Before Williams had filled out his first lineup card during spring training, he was involved in his first controversy. One of the problems he'd been wrestling with over the winter was what to do with the lead-off spot in his batting order. Damaso Garcia had been the Blue Jays' lead-off man for four seasons. On the surface he appeared to have the necessary tools: he was a good contact hitter with plenty of speed. But Garcia was a free swinger, not given to taking many walks. Hence, his on-base percentage was among the lowest of all lead-off men. In 1985, for example, despite a decent .282 batting average, his on-base percentage was just .302, the lowest of every lead-off man in the league. On his own team there were nine players with better on-base percentages.

The bottom line for a lead-off man is the number of runs he scores. In 1985 Garcia scored seventy runs, sixth best on the team. Williams, and many others in the organization, felt it was time to make a change.

The problem rested with Garcia's fierce pride. He relished his role as lead-off man, fancying himself the catalyst. Often he had been, but not often enough. It was clear that any change would be viewed as a demotion by the man.

But rather than ignore the situation and maintain the status quo, Williams made it clear from opening day that Lloyd Moseby was his choice to lead off. In retrospect, it is also clear that Garcia never really recovered from that blow to his ego. "For four years I was good enough to be the lead-off man," said Garcia. "Now in the fifth year all of a sudden I'm not good enough."

♦ ALEXANDER THE GRATE

Whatever the result, it was not a great starting point for spring training. Shortly thereafter, both Tom Filer and Gary Lavelle were sidelined with serious elbow problems, finishing their seasons before they had even begun.

Then, just before the end of spring training, there was more trouble in paradise: Doyle Alexander, who had won more games than any other Toronto pitcher over the previous two seasons, requested a trade. In preliminary contract extension talks with the Jays' front office, he was not satisfied that he figured prominently in their plans.

Through the early part of the season Alexander continued to goad team management, leaving Gillick no alternative but to find a taker or risk further disruptions by his disgruntled pitcher. On July 5, Bobby Cox said yes to a deal that would send Alexander to Atlanta in exchange for pitcher Duane Ward. But by that time there was already a lot of water under the Blue Jays' bridge.

Right from the beginning of the regular schedule the Jays were in trouble. Jimmy Key and Dave Stieb, expected to be the leaders of the starting rotation, both began the season in horrendous slumps. Key did not get his first win until May 9, Stieb not until May 30. Between them, in April, they started nine games and lasted a cumulative forty innings, allowing thirty-eight runs. That put a tremendous strain on the Toronto bull pen as the Jays sank to last place and stayed there for the entire month of May.

Since by the end of that month it was evident that Moseby's power was needed elsewhere in the lineup, Tony Fernandez was installed as the lead-off man on June 8. Over the course of the final 108 games of the season he hit .320 with nine homers and fifty-one RBIs.

But the season, from an offensive standpoint, belonged to the Killer Bees: Bell and Barfield. In the team's history only one man — Willie Upshaw, in 1983 — had ever driven in one hundred runs, but in 1986 both Bell and Barfield did it, each finishing with 108 RBIs to share the team record. Barfield led the major leagues with forty homers, while Bell hit thirty-one. Barfield hit .289, Bell .309. On defence, Barfield led the American League with twenty outfield assists, while Bell was right behind in second place with seventeen.

For each man, all the years of work had paid off.

♦ THE KILLER BEES

Jesse Lee Barfield was born in Joliet, Illinois, on October 29, 1959. Thousands of miles away, in San Pedro de Macoris, Dominican Republic, George Antonio Bell was already eight days old. Long before their careers converged on the outfield turf at Exhibition Stadium, they shared a common dream.

29

The Killer Bees, Jesse Barfield (left) *and George Bell* (above) *combined for 71 homers and 216 RBIs in 1986.*

George Bell, Lloyd Moseby and Jesse Barfield were born within two weeks of each other in the fall of 1959.

"I guess it's the same all over," said Barfield. "From the time I was about twelve, I wanted to be a ball player. It was all I wanted." Barfield was raised by his mother, Annie, the eldest of four children, and because of her vigilance he escaped many of the problems that plague kids growing up black and poor in the big city.

By chance, when Barfield was in high school, Bobby Mattick dropped by a game in which Barfield was playing. Mattick was there to see a pitcher from the other team named Bill Gullickson, but when Mattick left that afternoon, he took away notes on "that skinny kid" Barfield, who hit the double that won the game.

For two years after he was drafted and signed by the Jays in June, 1977, Barfield grappled with the hard realities of professional baseball. "I remember going up to the plate and the guy was throwing breaking pitches," he recalled. "I just flailed at that thing. I had no idea." He hit .226 with Utica of the New York Penn League that season, then .206 a year later with Dunedin of the Florida State League.

The next year, at Kinston of the Carolina League, some of the athletic promise that Mattick had seen started to become obvious. His hitting improved to .264 with eight homers and seventy-one RBIs. Two years later, at the tail end of his second year at Knoxville of the Southern League, Barfield got a taste of major-league life, batting .232 with a couple of September homers.

A year later he was in Toronto to stay. That's not to say he was always happy. Under Bobby Cox's strict platoon system it wasn't until 1985 that Barfield was allowed to go out and show his stuff every day. "That was frustrating," he says now. "But I had to live with it. I think I've proven all I needed was the opportunity."

Bell is the eldest of five children born to George and Juanita Bell in the town of Sante Fe, just outside San Pedro. George Sr. was a railroad engineer, ferrying locally grown sugar cane to the nearest seaport. Juanita ran a restaurant. "We always had plenty to eat," Bell says. "We weren't rich, but we lived okay."

Later, when he became a local hero, Bell made sure that some of the less fortunate children of his community had enough. He provided shoes and clothing to needy families, he made sure there were always flowers at the local hospital on Mother's Day and he was a major financial contributor to the local orphanage.

Bell was signed as a seventeen-year-old by the Phillies and sent to Helena, Montana, to get his feet wet in professional baseball. "My first year was terrible," he says. "The other players, both black and white, looked down on Latin players. It was a very lonely season."

A year later at Spartanburg he showed his first signs of the power he has today, hitting .305 with twenty-two homers and 102 RBIs. His 1980 season was a washout because of an injured shoulder, but already Pat Gillick was on the scent.

The Phils thought no one would notice Bell since he'd missed most of the season, so they left him unprotected for the major-league draft in December, 1980. Gillick spent $25,000 and drafted him. The Jays kept him on their roster in 1981, under stipulations of the draft rules.

In 1982 Bell was at Syracuse suffering through "the worst year of my life." After a series of injuries, including a pitched ball that hit him in the face and fractured his jaw, he considered quitting. "I was destroyed mentally. I was destroyed physically. I thought I was finished with baseball."

Of course he was not. By mid-1983 he was in Toronto and he's been tearing the cover off the ball ever since. In 1986 he stepped into the star category but it wasn't until 1987 that he took it another step farther, winning the American League MVP award.

◆ WE LIKE EICH

On June 1 the mighty Jays had won just twenty-three of forty-nine games. They trailed the streaking Boston Red Sox by eleven games. Over the course of the next three months, with Key back in form and Barfield and Bell having their best seasons, the Jays fought their way back into the race. From June 1 until September 1, they had the best record in the division, winning fifty-three of eighty-five games to pull within three and a half games of the leaders.

But after winning two of three against Cleveland to begin the month of September, the Jays hit a brick wall. They went to Chicago and lost two of three and looked bad doing it. Then they came home and were swept by the Yankees in a three-game series. By the time they had put a stop to the skid on September 12, they had fallen ten games behind.

"There were two turning points for us," said Williams in analyzing the season, "and they both came back-to-back. First there was the winning streak [nine games at the end of August] that got us close. Then there was the weekend in Chicago when our bats went cold. That led into the Yankee series, and we just went flat. But it all seemed to start in Chicago."

By the time the Jays went into Boston on Friday, September 26, the Red Sox needed just two wins to clinch the pennant. That night Jimmy Key squared off

Above: *Jesse Barfield entered the 1987 season as the defending major-league home run champion.*

Left: *Mark Eichhorn and his unorthodox submarine style confused opposition hitters in 1986.*

against Roger Clemens in what evolved into a twelve-inning thriller as the Jays won 1-0 on Jesse Barfield's home run over Fenway Park's Green Monster. The following afternoon Boston's Bruce Hurst outduelled Jim Clancy for a 2-0 victory and set the stage for Boston's clinching party on Sunday. They accomplished it in convincing fashion, whipping the Jays 12-3.

It had been a disappointing season, to be sure. The Jays won thirteen fewer games in 1986 than they did in '85. Some changes clearly needed to be made. But the season had not been a total bust. Aside from the emergence of Bell and Barfield as two of the game's top bashers, there was the sensational story of Mark Eichhorn, who came out of the woodwork to lead the overworked Toronto bull pen.

Eichhorn had been drafted in 1979 as a shortstop but quickly made the conversion to pitcher. After five years in the Jays organization, he was going nowhere fast and looking for a gimmick that would get him to the majors. He found it in the form of an unorthodox submarine delivery. He worked on it for a couple of seasons and then was invited to spring training in '86, "more or less as a guy to pitch batting practice," as Pat Gillick viewed the situation.

By the end of camp Eichhorn had impressed the staff so much they kept him on the team, and by the end of the season he had recorded some eyepopping numbers: fourteen wins, ten saves, an earned-run average of 1.72, sixty-nine appearances totalling 157 innings, 105 hits and just forty-five walks. He worked long relief. He worked short relief. Mostly, he worked.

"I shudder to think where we'd be without Eichhorn," said Williams.

♦ CLEANING HOUSE

Bill Caudill's days were numbered. In addition to the fact that his fastball had disappeared, there was the presence of Tom Henke to consider. Henke had accumulated twenty-seven saves in '86, and Caudill, by this time, was merely taking space on the roster. Before the 1987 season began, he was released.

It was time, also, for Garcia to move along. Before spring training he was traded to Atlanta where, in a season and a half, he played hardly at all because of knee and shoulder problems. Released in 1988, Garcia eventually landed a AAA job in the Dodgers organization.

Cliff Johnson was released near the end of the season; at age thirty-nine, his career was at an end. He had played eighteen years as a professional and had appeared with no less than seven different big-league teams. His twenty career pinch-hit home runs is a major-league record.

"We need to improve our speed and defence," said Williams, a sentiment echoed by Gillick. "It's a young man's game, and maybe we need to get some young legs out there." It was not, however, a time to make wholesale changes. Despite their inability to defend the division title, the Jays remained one of the potent forces in baseball. The nucleus — Bell, Barfield, Moseby, Fernandez, Whitt, Key, Stieb, Henke and Clancy — was evidence enough that the Jays would be a powerful unit in 1987.

1987

BEST OF TIMES, WORST OF TIMES

It was getting on towards four o'clock on the morning of May 21 when the change in pitch of the jet's whine signalled that Seattle was not far off. Four miles below, the black earth became a twinkling mirror-image of the star-filled sky as first Tacoma, then the larger expanse of Seattle filled the horizon. Aside from the occasional whoop from the card game at the back of the Blue Jays' charter flight, it was quiet as the players — some with their families aboard — tried to sleep.

Tom Henke spoke softly so as not to awaken his three-year-old daughter, Kimberly. While his huge right paw gently stroked her hair, his mind wandered to a moment four hours and a thousand miles previous when a bat wielded by Wally Joyner, the superb young first baseman of the California Angels, had collided with a Henke fastball to put an abrupt end to a three-game series between the Blue Jays and the Angels.

Joyner's decisive home run was struck in the bottom of the tenth inning with the score tied 4-4. Six weeks into the season Henke had finally given up a run. The loss was a bitter pill to swallow for the Jays, especially in light of their overcoming a three-run California lead in the ninth inning.

"You can't let it get to you," said Henke. "You just can't. The game can eat you up if you give in to second-guessing yourself. I threw a good pitch, and he hit it. It's gonna happen plenty more times, too. You play this game long enough, and you're going to experience every emotional extreme you can imagine — the thrill of victory and the agony of defeat.

"We've got a long way to go this year. Nobody knows where it'll lead, but I know this: we'll have some good times and some bad times. We just can't let ourselves get too high or too low."

By the 1987 season Tom Henke had established himself as one of the dominant relief pitchers in baseball.

Henke knew about good times and bad times. He had blossomed relatively late in life for a pitcher, knocking around in the Texas Rangers' chain for years without success. He returned each off-season to his roots in Taos, a hamlet of some 700 people nestled in the foothills of the Ozark Mountains in southern Missouri.

Life in the Rangers' chain was not easy for Henke, who found himself on the wrong side of manager Doug Rader. At the end of the 1984 season the Rangers signed free agent Cliff Johnson away from the Blue Jays. As compensation the Jays were allowed to select a player from a pool of unprotected major-leaguers. When their turn came, they selected Henke.

After an impressive spring in 1985, Henke went to Syracuse as bull-pen insurance in case something happened to Bill Caudill. By midseason the Jays needed Henke desperately and he delivered. By season's end they were writing songs about him and calling him "The Terminator" in Toronto.

Back in Taos, across the street from Doug's Service Station and Bar, on the bulletin board outside Eikins Food Store, the exploits of Tom Henke were chronicled. Since the town had no newspaper and word of Tom's exploits was hard to come by, clippings from Toronto newspapers were eagerly awaited and dutifully posted.

♦ LIMP AND DRAINED

On that spring morning in 1987 no one could have foreseen the tumult of the months to come. When it was all over on October 4, two baseball teams and two cities — Detroit and Toronto — would be drained and limp after one of the most nerve-snapping, energy-sapping pennant races in history.

Through 1987 the Jays were a model of consistency, jockeying with the Yankees, Milwaukee and finally Detroit at the top of the standings. From the third week of the season on they never fell lower than third place. They won twelve games in April, sixteen in May, seventeen in June, fifteen in July and seventeen in August and then came pounding down the stretch with fierce determination, only to hit a brick wall with seven games to go after already winning nineteen games in September.

Each month produced its new batch of heroes, led always by George Bell. April and May belonged to Bell (sixteen homers, forty-two RBIs) and Barfield (twelve homers, twenty-four RBIs). In June, Fernandez climbed aboard that bandwagon, hitting .353. In July, as Barfield tailed off, a host of support came from people like Ernie Whitt, Fred McGriff and Rance Mulliniks.

Questions that had lingered through training camp — Dave Stieb's elbow? Second base? Middle relief? Bench strength? — all began to sort themselves out.

After a short struggle Stieb found his form and contributed almost as the Stieb of old would have. The Mike Sharperson experiment at second base ended just a few days after that evening flight into Seattle, when the team management decided he couldn't do the job.

Iorg and Manny Lee handled the assignment there until August, when Nelson Liriano was promoted to not only second base, but the lead-off spot in the line-up, as well.

Garth Iorg, a survivor of the 1977 expansion draft, completed his career in 1987.

Charlie Moore became the right-handed hitting catcher, adding experience and versatility to the bench. Juan Beniquez came later to give the same support in the outfield.

Jim Clancy and Jimmy Key were the constants in a pitching staff that led the league in earned-run average from the very beginning. Key led the American League in earned-run average and finished a close second to Roger Clemens in the voting for the Cy Young award. John Cerutti, in his role as a spot starter and midreliever, rattled off eight consecutive wins, a streak sandwiched on both ends by losses to Oakland's Dave Stewart.

And then there was Henke, night after night, to slam the door. In the end he led the league in saves and became a rarity: a long shot Cy Young candidate who did not win a single game all year.

♦ BELL AT THE CENTRE

Because of Bell's dominance, there was always a tendency to believe he was

John Cerutti proved a valuable member of the Toronto pitching staff. His resilient arm allowed him to both start and relieve.

carrying the team on his own. There is no question he was there more than anyone. He hit forty-seven home runs and drove in 134 runs while hitting for a .308 average. But his emergence as the league's number-one slugger should not cast too long a shadow on the daily contributions of his teammates.

"I'm proud of the season I've had," said Bell, "but I'm just one guy. Nobody in baseball does it all himself. When the season is over, then I can look back at the numbers and say, 'Hey, that was pretty good,' but if we don't win, it doesn't mean anything."

There were the inevitable lows and highs: a disappointing 15-14 defeat at the hands of the Yankees in the wild and woolly opener of a Canada Day series in Toronto; and that memorable night when the Jays shattered the major-league record with ten home runs in one game against Baltimore in September.

When it was over, Bell was named the league's most valuable player, but he will always be haunted by his inability to deliver during the last two weeks of the season when the Jays and the Tigers hooked up in a classic confrontation that would dwarf the drama of the World Series.

◆ A HEAVYWEIGHT TITLE FIGHT

We take you now to Exhibition Stadium, September 24, 1987. When last they met the Blue Jays, seventy-four days previous, the Tigers were simply a team trying to survive. They were well back in the pack, slowly recovering ground lost when they started the season by winning just eleven of their first thirty games. Still, after the Jays won two of three in that June series at Tiger Stadium, Detroit was third, six games behind.

By mid-August the Tigers had rallied past the Yankees, taking dead aim at the Jays. For the next forty games the Jays and the Tigers measured each other from afar, often thousands of miles apart but rarely out of mind. The two rivals were never more than one and a half games apart at the top of the standings from August 12 until this day.

On that cool September morning the Jays and the Tigers awoke in the same city for the first time in three months. The Jays had flown home from Baltimore and a three-game sweep of the Orioles, arriving just past 2:00 a.m. An hour later the Tigers came in from Boston, where they had won two of three from the Red Sox, still trailing Toronto by a scant half game.

Less than two weeks remained in the season. Toronto had ten games remaining, Detroit eleven. But each knew the season would be decided in the seven games in which they faced each other. But neither team could have envisioned just how dramatically the scene would unfold.

The tension at Exhibition Stadium that evening was palpable. Sensing something special about to happen, the international baseball media filled the press box to capacity.

"This is perfect for baseball," said Toronto reliever Tom Henke, sensing the moment. "It's like a World Series before the season even ends — two of baseball's best teams playing seven games to determine the champion. Yeah, this is good. Real good."

Appropriately, two of the decade's top pitchers prepared to face each other. Flanagan, a Blue Jay for only twenty-five days but a veteran of dozens of crucial situations in his twelve-year career, would test his mettle against Jack Morris, the premier pitcher in the American League during the 1980s. Ironically, this promising matchup became a minor footnote in the evening's events, which shaped the course of the series.

There was no score in the third inning when, with Detroit's Bill Madlock on first, Toronto second baseman Nelson Liriano fielded a sharply hit ground ball from the bat of Kirk Gibson, snapping the throw to Tony Fernandez at second base. Brushing the base with his foot, Fernandez stepped to the right-field side of the bag as he relayed to first. But Madlock was coming in hard. In his determination to break up the double play, he ignored the base entirely, sliding headlong at Fernandez' knees. The shortstop flipped up and over Madlock, crashing to earth on the seam that divides the turf playing field from the dirt around second base. He landed not on the padded playing surface but on a metal border. His elbow was broken, his season finished.

"Sheik" Jose Nunez reviews a disappointing game.

Two hours later, when Ernie Whitt bounded home from third base on a Morris wild pitch in the eighth inning to give Toronto a 4-3 win, Fernandez was on the operating table at Mount Sinai Hospital. His loss cast a pall over the Blue Jays clubhouse, despite this most important victory. The prevailing sense, prophetic in nature, was that the Jays had won the battle but lost the war. At this most crucial part of the season Toronto would have to go on without the man many believed to be their most valuable player.

♦ SPOTLIGHT ON LEE

Chapter Two in this remarkable story unfolded the next night. With Fernandez gone, young Manuel Lora Lee found himself squarely in the spotlight. Both Fernandez and Lee grew up in San Pedro de Macoris in the Dominican Republic, a town that exports sugar cane and major-league ball players. They specialize in shortstops. In fact, at one point several years ago no less than seven of the twenty-six starting shortstops in the majors were from San Pedro. And if Fernandez is the best their town has ever produced, Lee is not far behind.

The road to Toronto had not been as well paved for Lee as it was for Fernandez. His offensive skills simply did not measure up to his consummate defence. But on that night the constant struggle was forgotten. It was Manny Lee's turn.

In this second game Detroit left-hander Frank Tanana held his usual mastery over the Blue Jays. He was pitching a shutout after seven innings, but Tigers manager Sparky Anderson decided to open the eighth with reliever Dickie Noles on the mound. Noles pitched one uneventful inning but gave up a one-out single in the ninth to Jesse Barfield.

Pinch hitter Rick Leach drilled relief pitcher Willie Hernandez' second offering into right field for a double, putting runners at second and third for Lee, still with one out. Before you could say "a star is born," Lee had sliced the first pitch he saw down the right-field line for a game-tying triple. Still with one out, Anderson ordered his next reliever, Mike Henneman, to walk two hitters intentionally, to load the bases and set up a forced play at home, while also keeping the double-play option open.

Lloyd Moseby drilled a hot grounder to Lou Whitaker at second. Eschewing the double play, he tried to cut off the run at the plate, but a moment's indecision preceded an errant throw and the game was over. Toronto had won 3-2.

♦ A ONE-RUN SQUEAKER

The third game of the series was a wild affair that saw Toronto come back from a 9-4 deficit to win 10-9 on Juan Beniquez' dramatic three-run double in the bottom of the ninth. For the first time since the Fernandez injury, the Jays dared to hope his absence would not be so devastating as first feared. After all, they had won three games without him and had the Tigers on the ropes.

The Tigers were a veteran team, a team difficult to rattle. But clearly this third one-run loss in a row had them shaken. "We've got one more chance," said Anderson, "with Doyle [Alexander] pitching. Oh, my God, if we lose that one, we have no control. None."

With but seven games remaining in the regular schedule, Toronto held a commanding three-and-a-half-game lead. Kirk Gibson, the gruff outfielder and perennial clutch player, tried to bluff it out and in the process offered this prescient statement: "Maybe the Jays should enjoy it while they can. Maybe we're setting the biggest bear trap of all time. It's not our nature to roll over."

Still, after that game, the enormous odds were not lost upon the Detroit team. As afternoon turned into evening and evening into night, a group of them remained in the clubhouse talking baseball, trying to screw up their confidence to come back strongly on Sunday. "It was as if nobody wanted to be alone," recalled Darrell Evans much later. "We needed each other and we needed to collect ourselves."

The Sunday game against Alexander and the Tigers was as emotionally charged as any in the Blue Jays' history, perhaps even as electric as the 1985 playoffs. As if the anticipation of sweeping Detroit and locking up the division title was not enough, there was the return of Alexander to consider. Fifteen months previous Alexander's carefully orchestrated campaign to be traded away from Toronto had been rewarded with a deal that sent him to the Atlanta Braves for Duane Ward. Many fans objected to his methods. In August the Tigers needed pitching help for the stretch run, and Atlanta GM Bobby Cox obliged, sending them Alexander for minor-league prospect John Smoltz. Alexander was unbeatable in Tiger stripes, and on this Sunday he strode to the mound with an unblemished 8-0 record to face his old teammates. No player who visited Exhibition Stadium has ever been accorded such a derisive welcome.

Injuries to Ernie Whitt and Tony Fernandez dealt a blow to Toronto's division-title hopes. Fernandez (bottom) *broke his throwing elbow trying to elude the slide of Detroit's Bill Madlock. Five days later, Whitt's ribs were fractured in a second-base collision with Milwaukee's Paul Molitor* (top).

♦ GIBSON'S BLAST

Of course, Alexander was oblivious to the more than 43,000 fans. He gave up a run in the first inning, then he and Clancy went toe-to-toe until the ninth. That's when Gibson redirected relief ace Tom Henke's fastball over the fence in deep right to tie the game.

Extra innings. Evans gave Detroit a 2-1 lead with a solo homer against Jeff Musselman in the eleventh, but the Jays counterpunched in the bottom of the frame, Jesse Barfield delivering a two-out, RBI single. But in the thirteenth inning Gibson came calling again, looping a single into short centre field to score Jim Walewander with the decisive run.

The Tigers went home for a four-game series against the Baltimore Orioles, and the Jays were left to contend with the tough Milwaukee Brewers in a three-game set. But the events of the previous weekend had obviously left each of the front-runners drained. Detroit could manage only a split with the sad-sack Orioles, while Toronto went down to a devastating three-game sweep at the hands of the Brewers.

♦ COOKED GOOSE

Worse than the sweep was the fact that catcher Ernie Whitt would not be available for the Detroit series. He had suffered a broken rib in a second-base collision with Brewers' Paul Molitor.

On Thursday evening, with the Tigers preparing for their final game against the Orioles at Tiger Stadium, the Blue Jays congregated at Pearson International Airport to board their charter flight to Windsor with a bus connection to their Dearborn, Michigan, hotel. As the jet rose, there was a loud bang from an engine on the left side of the aircraft, the result of a Canada goose being sucked into the huge turbine. The team returned to the terminal, unnerved. While they waited, several coaches and players listened to the Detroit game on the radio, and by the time the plane was ready for takeoff again, it was apparent that Toronto's lead had slipped to one game.

As the team filed back onto the aircraft, George Bell turned to a flight attendant and asked, "What's the meal? Cooked goose?"

Three games remained in the regular season. To be champions, the Tigers needed to win all three. Two wins would force a playoff.

In the first game it was again Alexander against Clancy. With Toronto's big bats — George Bell, Jesse Barfield and Rance Mulliniks — suddenly silent, it was Manny Lee who stunned Alexander with a three-run homer to stake Clancy to an early 3-0 lead. But the Tigers rallied for two runs in the third inning, two more in the fourth, and that's the way it stayed for a 4-3 Detroit victory. With two games remaining the teams were tied.

Saturday afternoon was a rematch of the opening game pitchers, Flanagan and Morris, and this time they took centre stage and would not give it up. Morris

Above: *On the final day of the 1987 season, base runners were few for the Blue Jays. Here, Lloyd Moseby is stranded at second base in the first inning.*

Left: *Not even a most-valuable-player season could console George Bell.*

left after nine innings, the score tied 2-2. He punctuated his superb afternoon by striking out Moseby and Mulliniks to end the ninth.

"It was pure adrenalin at that point," said Morris. "I knew my season could be over. There was no reason to save anything."

Flanagan stayed on through eleven and almost had to be dragged from the mound. "When you're in a groove like that, you feel like you can pitch forever," he said.

With one out in the twelfth, the Tigers loaded the bases against Jeff Musselman, and then, with the infield drawn in, Alan Trammell drilled a ball that went between Lee's legs to score the winning run.

Now, after 161 games, Detroit had a one-game lead, and the Jays needed a win on Sunday to force a sudden-death playoff on Monday.

Despite the difficult situation, there was no sense of despondency in the Blue Jays' clubhouse. Instead, there was more a feeling of awe among the players.

"That," said Musselman, "was the best baseball I've ever seen."

♦ A ROUTINE FLY BALL

In the eyes of many baseball fans Tiger Stadium is to baseball parks what St. Peter's is to cathedrals. And it was to this shrine that thousands were drawn early on Sunday morning. The corner of Michigan and Trumbull was a carnival of sight and sound. Inside, a changeable wind was blowing moderately out to left field, a factor that would bear heavily on the game's outcome.

In the bottom of the second inning Detroit's Larry Herndon lifted a lazy fly ball to left field. Toronto pitcher Jimmy Key wheeled to watch George Bell catch it. Routine. Bell moved a few steps back. Now another step. Two more. And then Bell watched in frantic disbelief as the ball settled into the second row of seats.

"I didn't hit it very good," said Herndon, a man of few words.

"I thought it was just another out," said Key.

And that's the way it ended, a 1-0 shutout for Tanana and a division championship for the Tigers, who would soon bow out quietly against the Minnesota Twins in the American League Championship Series, emotionally and physically pummelled from their struggle against the Blue Jays.

Through the next weeks and months, there was much finger pointing and amateur analysis of the Blue Jays' collapse, but the answers were simple: injuries to Fernandez and Whitt were simply too much for the Blue Jays' offence to bear. Bell tried to carry the team and in the process became an easy out for Detroit pitchers who refused to offer him anything he could hit. By doing that, the Tigers eliminated the heart of the Toronto batting order, short-circuiting one of the premier offences in baseball.

It was a disappointing end to a season of such promise. More than that, it raised a major question in fans' minds: Could the Jays rebound in 1988?

Franklin

1988

A SUMMER OF DISCONTENT

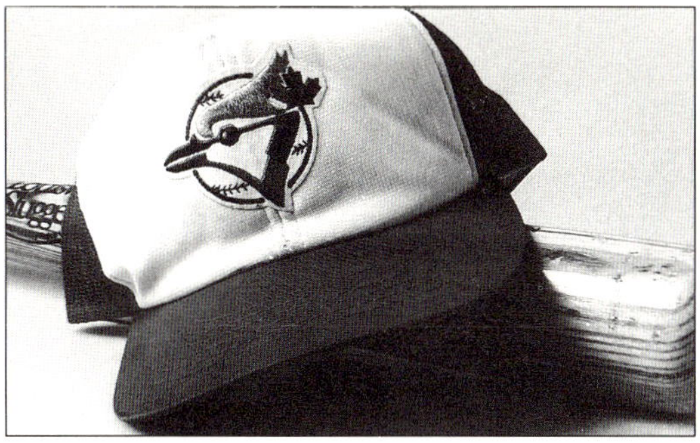

A baseball team is a very fragile thing. You start with talent, then add equal parts youth, experience, attitude, trust, confidence and luck. Then you cross your fingers. When one or more of those elements falls out of balance with the others, the entire structure can come tumbling down like a house of cards as it did in 1988 for the Jays.

Years from now people will look back on the 1988 standings in the American League East Division and marvel at what a race to the wire it must have been. Boston with eighty-nine wins, Detroit with eighty-eight, Toronto and Milwaukee with eighty-seven, New York with eighty-five. In fact, it was not much of a race. Not even a light jog, really. By the middle of September the Red Sox had control and eventually clinched the pennant despite losing six of their last seven games.

It was an especially exasperating season for the Blue Jays, a season remembered for bitterness and controversy that began in Florida and dogged them through the summer. When it was over, it was easy to target as many as a dozen games that could have turned the tide. Injuries, attitude and pure bad luck conspired against the team.

By the time spring training began late in February, 1988, signs of trouble were as plentiful as Canadian licence plates in Dunedin. Five players had undergone off-season surgical procedures. Some were considered minor, but as Jesse Barfield said on the day he arrived, "It's only minor surgery when it's done to somebody else."

Smiles were rare from George Bell in 1988. Even before training camp began, he was at odds with manager Jimy Williams.

♦ ADDING INSULTS TO INJURY

Barfield had had a wrist and a knee surgically repaired, and while he came to camp with a brave face, he was not nearly rehabilitated. In addition to his famous broken elbow, Tony Fernandez had undergone arthroscopic knee surgery in October. Ditto for Willie Upshaw and relief pitcher Duane Ward.

The most serious case was pitcher Jeff Musselman, who had been targeted to join the Jays' starting rotation after a strong rookie season in the bull pen. In December, rotator-cuff damage to his pitching shoulder had been repaired. He would not be ready until June at least.

These things were already weighing on manager Jimy Williams' mind when Hurricane George hit the Blue Jays clubhouse and laid it flat.

During the off-season the Jays had attempted to do some long-range planning that they believed would help both offensively and defensively. In this plan George Bell would be the designated hitter. Lloyd Moseby would move to left field from centre. Rob Ducey and Sil Campusano would compete for Moseby's old job in centre.

"The plan had a lot of pluses, we felt," said Williams later. "First and foremost, it would take away some of the threat to Bell's knees and give him the best kind of offensive exposure. We wanted to get him 700 plate appearances under optimum circumstances. By not having to go to the outfield and run on the hard turf and dive for balls, we felt it would be easier on his sore knees. I don't want to be down on my knees, praying for his knees. Secondly, we felt that it would improve our defence."

But Bell, proud and stubborn, was having none of it. Six weeks before camp opened, Williams, Pat Gillick and several others from the Blue Jays office sat down with Bell at a meeting in Dallas and explained the plan. Bell's agents, Randall and Alan Hendricks, were in the process of negotiating a contract for Bell, the most valuable player in the American League in 1987. When the Blue Jays people left the meeting, they felt Bell understood what they wanted. Bell had a different view.

"In Dallas," said Bell, "[Williams] told me '10-15 games at DH,' and I agreed with him because that would be good for my legs. But not every day."

Moseby was also upset about the plan but, after signing a contract extension upon arrival at camp, said he would give left field a try. "I don't mind playing left," he said unconvincingly, "as long as people don't throw rocks at me. And it may be George throwing them."

Although the collective bargaining agreement said players didn't have to report until March 2, the Jays, like most other teams, had asked all players to be in camp by February 27 to prepare for their first exhibition game March 4. Bell, who had recently signed a two-year, $4-million contract, did not arrive until March 2, a signal that trouble was brewing.

And the day he arrived, he immediately lashed out verbally at Williams, setting the tone for training camp, an ugly tone that would dominate well into the season.

"There's gonna be a bomb explode," said Bell. "They think that just because they pay me a lot of money, they can make me do whatever they want. Well, they can't."

To Dave Perkins, of *The Toronto Star*, Bell said, "We'll see who lasts longer around here, Jimy Williams or me."

After a stormy meeting with Bell, Williams said, "I can't promise smooth sailing. Actions speak louder than words, and I just hope George goes out on the field and does his job."

On March 17, Williams pencilled in Bell's name as DH for a game in Dunedin against the Boston Red Sox. When Bell was called to the plate to lead off the second inning, he did not move from his seat in the bull pen down the left field line. A pinch hitter was sent to the plate while Bell and Williams repaired to the clubhouse for another shouting match. Bell was suspended.

♦ ANOTHER BLOWUP

An uneasy truce was reached after Randy Hendricks rushed to his client's side. Hurricane George had been downgraded to a tropical storm by the end of training camp, but untold damage had been wreaked on the team's collective psyche.

But if there was a problem, it was hard to identify on opening day. As the season began in Kansas City, Bell gave new meaning to the words "designated hitter." His first three times to the plate Bell smashed home runs, setting a major-league record for homers on opening day.

Ten games into the season, however, with a 4-6 record, Campusano struggling and team morale at a low ebb, Williams scrapped the entire experiment in hopes it would ease tensions.

But by Tuesday, July 26, Bell had hit just eleven more homers and was well off his forty-seven-homer pace of a year previous. Worse yet, the team was struggling along in sixth place, ten games behind the leading Detroit Tigers. On that night in Minneapolis, after Bell committed his sixth error in seven games, Williams removed him from the game, and the two had a heated argument in the dugout. For the next four days Bell was benched.

More words were exchanged, both in private and in the press.

"I respect him," said Williams of Bell, "but things will never be the same between George and me. It can't be repaired."

While the conflict between Williams and Bell got the headlines, there were plenty of other reasons for the Jays' substandard first half. Most important, Jimmy Key, the linchpin of the pitching staff, had been missing since the fifth week of the season when he had some bone chips surgically removed from his elbow. Jim Clancy got off to a terrible start, losing eleven of his first fifteen decisions. Mike Flanagan was inconsistent. Of the starters, only Dave Stieb had a strong first half. His 10-5 record with a 2.95 ERA sent him to the all-star game for the sixth time.

Barfield was struggling as he never had before in his career, batting .209 at the break. Ernie Whitt had only four homers and was hitting .220. And Tony Fernandez was clearly not yet fully recovered from his broken elbow and the surgery on his knee. Nelson Liriano, who had been handed the job at second base, was not playing up to standard, and Moseby, his chronically sore back giving him problems, was struggling at the plate and in the field.

There were, in fact, only a handful of bright spots through the early months of the season.

Kelly Gruber, who had been slated to platoon with Rance Mulliniks at third base, had stepped into an everyday role when Mulliniks injured a knee in the club's home opener against New York. Gruber had responded to his expanded job description in spectacular fashion, hitting .302 with eleven homers and a team-leading fifty-three RBIs by the all-star break and fielding his position perhaps better than any other third baseman in the American League.

Over at first base a legend was in the making.

♦ A BIG-LEAGUE TATER MAN

Born and raised a few miles across the bay from Dunedin in Tampa, Fred McGriff had been given only a slight chance to make the Blue Jays in the spring of 1987. Despite declining production from Willie Upshaw, the Jays' management had decided to give Upshaw another chance at first base.

But McGriff simply would not go quietly back to Syracuse. He had spent two full seasons at AAA already and didn't want to go back. He didn't. That spring he poled seven homers, spiced with a couple of tape measure shots that have since become a trademark. At six feet three inches and 215 pounds, with the shoulders of a blacksmith and the waist of a dancer, McGriff provided an imposing sight for pitchers.

He had spent the 1987 season sharing the role of designated hitter with Cecil Fielder. McGriff faced the right-handers, Fielder the lefties. McGriff parlayed that tandem into a team record for home runs by a rookie. He hit twenty of

Far left: *In 1988 Fred McGriff established himself as one of the game's most feared young sluggers, but baseball insiders were also impressed with his defence.*

Near left: *Off-season wrist surgery left Jesse Barfield in a weakened condition. His disappointing 1988 season had him looking for answers in all the wrong places.*

Right: *Kelly Gruber's improved play was one of few positive developments during the 1988 season.*

them, including one mammoth shot in New York against Yankee pitcher Rick Rhoden.

Under a different set of circumstances, McGriff might have been playing at Yankee Stadium on a regular basis. McGriff had originally been selected by New York (ninth round, 233rd overall) out of Tampa's Jefferson High in the 1981 amateur draft.

As a youngster, McGriff had not been terribly impressive as a ball player but there was no questioning his dream. The Cincinnati Reds trained not far from the McGriff home, and he was, as he said himself, "always over there, rooting around in the garbage cans after broken bats or trying to scavenge a baseball or two." Jefferson's coach, Pop Cuesta, remembers a gangly grade-ten student who was "small, weak and wore glasses."

In fact, Cuesta cut McGriff from the team that year because he felt the kid would benefit more from another season of Little League. But by his senior year he was a mainstay at Jefferson and had created an impression that endured. Six years later McGriff's uniform number was retired in a ceremony at the school.

His first professional year with the Yankees was not much to write home about. He hit just .148 in the rookie league. But his second season was more promising, producing nine homers and a .272 batting average. The Blue Jays' scouting staff took notice. When Pat Gillick was dealing away reliever Dale Murray to the Yankees in the winter of 1982, essentially for Dave Collins, he asked that McGriff be thrown in.

One spring day in 1984, when Collins saw McGriff for the first time at training camp, he stood beside the batting cage and silently watched as the young slugger launched majestic shots out of the Englebert Complex in Dunedin. Finally, Collins turned and said, to no one in particular, "I'd just like to know one thing: which one of us was the throw-in?"

During his 1987 apprenticeship one aspect of McGriff's development that impressed the coaching staff more than anything was his patience, which allowed him to draw more than his share of walks. "Fred McGriff is unique in that he has such a great eye for the strike zone," said batting coach Cito Gaston. "The word is getting around the league that you have to throw him strikes. You can't get him to go fishing. The umpires are beginning to realize that he's a student of the strike zone. When he lays off close ones, they take a good look, too. Unlike a lot of young power hitters, Fred has discipline. That discipline will take him a long, long way."

By the start of the 1988 season McGriff had taken over first base on a permanent basis. Upshaw, a team leader for most of the decade, had been traded to Cleveland. All McGriff did in 1988 was contend for the league home-run lead most of the season, finishing with thirty-four, second to Oakland's Jose Canseco.

But while Gruber and McGriff were emerging as cornerstones for the future, the team was as flat as yesterday's draft beer. Most of the season they were either fifth or sixth in the division, wallowing in mediocrity. Only the pathetic Baltimore Orioles kept Toronto from sinking to last place. The Jays were maddeningly consistent from April through August, never falling further than eight games under .500, but never rising more than three games above it, either.

The frustration for all concerned was magnified as it became apparent that no team seemed capable of running away with the American League East pennant. Finally in September the Jays caught fire.

They started the month three games under .500 and ten and a half games behind the first-place (and fading) Tigers, then proceeded to record the best month's work in team history, winning twenty-two of their final twenty-nine games to finish tantalizingly close.

♦ BELIEVE IT OR NOT

No player in baseball wrote a more remarkable final chapter to the regular season than did Dave Stieb, whose final two starts of the season were material that not even *Ripley's Believe It or Not* would touch.

In Cleveland on September 23, a Friday, Stieb started mowing down the Indians right from the start. By the time he got to the ninth, no Cleveland batter had made it to first base. Two more went down in the ninth before Julio Franco came to the plate. No Toronto pitcher had ever thrown a no-hitter, but it appeared Stieb was going to be the first. The count on Franco went to two balls and two strikes before he hit a bouncer directly at Manny Lee, the Toronto second baseman. Just as Lee was about to field the ball, it took a crazy hop off the dirt and over his head for a single.

Having survived that heartbreak with a "that's the story of my life" shrug, Stieb went to work on the Baltimore Orioles at Exhibition Stadium exactly one

In his final two starts of the season, Dave Stieb had good reason to wonder if "someone up there" had something against him. In both starts he lost no-hit bids with two outs in the ninth inning.

week later in his final start of the season. Again he was unhittable into the ninth. And again he got the twenty-fifth and twenty-sixth outs without difficulty. That brought Jim Traber to the plate. Again Stieb ran the count to two balls and two strikes. And again he had his heart broken. Traber fisted the next pitch, "a nasty slider, down and inside," just over the outstretched glove of Fred McGriff into right field for a single.

Fifty years previous, Johnny Vander Meer of the Cincinnati Reds had pitched back-to-back no-hitters against the Braves and the Dodgers, but Dave Stieb's two near misses in succession may be even tougher to duplicate.

Toronto finished up with a six-game winning streak, but there were easily a dozen games the Jays could look back upon and say "If only . . . ."

"You can look back all you want," said Williams. "You can say 'if' all you want, but it always comes out to eighty-seven wins. And that just wasn't enough."

No one had felt the weight of the season on his shoulders more than the manager, who had now completed his third year at the helm. Over the course of those years only two managers in baseball — Detroit's Sparky Anderson and Davey Johnson of the Mets — had more wins than Jimy Williams. Yet throughout the season fans and media alike seemed united in their desire to have him fired.

But when the season was finished, Williams was rehired for a fourth season, a clear message that the inmates were not running the asylum.

Jimy Williams and first base coach Billy Smith said goodbye to their fans after the final game of 1988, the last full season the Blue Jays played in Exhibition Stadium.

♦ FAREWELL TO CNE

Williams survived, but the future of Exhibition Stadium is not so certain. The original grandstand was constructed 110 years ago and has gone through a variety of changes in its rich history. But baseball is and will be its lasting legacy.

It was a terrible baseball facility with few redeeming qualities. That goes without debate. Dave Stieb once volunteered to "come around and help if they decide to reduce this place to a pile of bricks." No doubt there are scores of pitchers who would join him to dismantle what was clearly a hitter's park.

Regardless, it was home sweet home. In the early days players complained that the fans were too quiet, too polite. Given the team's dismal early record, that may have been a blessing. But as the team improved, the fans became more animated and forever loyal. Even some pitchers have fond memories of the ugly old joint.

"I'll remember the first time I walked to the mound before the Toronto fans," says Tom Henke. "I started out the season in Syracuse, and then I came up and got a couple of wins right away in Baltimore. Then we came here, and in my first appearance I got a standing ovation. That'll stick in my mind for the rest of my life. It was unbelievable. The fans had never seen me before, but they were pumped up."

"When you think back," said Jimy Williams, "whether you laugh or you cry, you can't replace the memories. There have been some crazy times. People should hang on to their memorabilia. It's going to be really valuable someday."

The Jays return in 1989 but only as tourists. Never again will a baseball season end at Exhibition Stadium. The old lady of the midway has had her day.